SALVATION IN MY POCKET

Salvation in My Pocket

FRAGMENTS OF
FAITH AND THEOLOGY

BENJAMIN MYERS

CASCADE *Books* • Eugene, Oregon

SALVATION IN MY POCKET
Fragments of Faith and Theology

Copyright © 2013 Benjamin Myers. All rights reserved. Except for brief quotations in critical publications or reviews, no part of this book may be reproduced in any manner without prior written permission from the publisher. Write: Permissions. Wipf and Stock Publishers, 199 W. 8th Ave., Suite 3, Eugene, OR 97401.

Cascade Books
An Imprint of Wipf and Stock Publishers
199 W. 8th Ave., Suite 3
Eugene, OR 97401

www.wipfandstock.com

ISBN 13: 978-60899-757-2

Cataloguing-in-Publication Data

Myers, Benjamin, 1978–

    Salvation in my pocket : fragments of faith and theology / Benjamin Myers.

    x + 146 p. ; 23 cm. Includes index.

    ISBN 13: 978-1-60899-757-2

    1. Theology—blogs. 2. Blogs—Religious aspects—Christianity. I. Title.

BR115 M94 2013

Manufactured in the U.S.A.

Photo detail of Chagall's *American Windows* © 2013 Sharon Mollerus, used under a Creative Commons Attribution-Commercial license:http://creativecommons.org/licenses/by/2.0/deed.en

To Felicity, Anna, and James,
who teach me more than all the books

> There is a light, a step, a call
> This evening on the Orange Tree.

—John Shaw Neilson, "The Orange Tree" (1919)

Contents

Preface ix

I. FASTING AND FEASTING

Amen 3
Arms 6
Berlin 8
Blue 10
Books 12
Boredom 13
Breakfast 15
California 16
Catechesis 22
Childhood 25
Circus 28
Cross 33
Curls 37
Drawing 42
Face 45
Feast 48
Forgiven 51
German 54
Grandfather 57
Horses 58
Ice Cream 59
Joy 67

II. HOW THE LIGHT GETS IN

Ladies 73
Libraries 75
Love 79
Manager 82

Mega 83
Mistake 85
Pan 86
Pocket 89
Prayer 90
Priest 93
Psalms 94
Revelation 96
Sacrifice 100
Saints 101
Showing 103
Smile 106
Song 110
Sydney 111

III. YOUNGER THAN THAT NOW

Theft 115
Theologians 117
Theophany 119
Thirty-Three 120
Thumbs 122
Tigers 123
Time 124
Together 126
Violence 127
Virgin 129
Water 131
Words (I) 133
Words (II) 134
Writing 135
Year 139

Epilogue 141
Index 143

Preface

The teaching of Christianity is that God is interested in ordinary human lives. God created human beings—these lovely, tragic creatures, so prone to delirious happiness and extravagant misfortune—and was very charmed by them. And so God became a creature like us, in order to get a better look at us and to see things from our point of view. And, if possible, to mend our broken ways. Because of this—because of the incarnation—we are able to confess that God is interested in us and that everything in our world is somehow related to God.

To believe all this is to see at the bottom of things not human struggles or agendas, not human power and agency, but a simple act of divine giving. It is to see all things against a backdrop of inexhaustible divine generosity, and even the most ordinary daily circumstances as occasions for joy.

The short pieces assembled in this book are miniature experiments in joy. They are attempts to express some of the difference God makes to ordinary experience, and to discover glimpses of God's generosity in everyday life. Most of these pieces were written originally for the blog Faith & Theology (faith-theology.com). Others have appeared here and there in various magazines and websites, and I have added several new pieces that have not appeared before. "Showing" was first published in *I Believe in God*, edited by William W. Emilsen (North Parramatta, NSW: UTC, 2011). I would like to record my thanks to the online community at Faith & Theology, a community that has given rise to much writing and many friendships over the past several years. My thanks are due especially to Kim Fabricius, who has been a constant encouragement, as well as an influence—thank him or blame him—on the aphoristic style adopted in many of these reflections. I also thank Steve Wright, who provided invaluable assistance in preparing the manuscript.

If there is any thread that holds these haphazard reflections together, it is just the conviction that beneath the surface of things there lurks an invitation, gentle and alluring; that even in sadness and misfortune there is always rising up, as if from hidden wells, the promise of peace; and that the final word spoken over this world, and over each human life, will be a word of joy.

Sydney
Feast of All Saints, 2012

I. Fasting and Feasting

Amen

Our father who art in heaven

Without prayer there is only—myself. Between the heaven of prayer and the hell of the self there is no middle way.

Hallowed be thy name

Prayer does not give me what I want. It pummels my wants, kneads them, stretches them my whole life long, until at the last hour of my life I have learned to want one thing only, the only thing worth having. And so my whole life becomes a hidden sigh, an inarticulate utterance of the Name of God. My death will be my prayer, the sigh by which I give myself up at last into the presence of the Name.

Thy kingdom come

My prayer encompasses not my own life only but the entire world of which I am a part. What defines this world is scarcity, injustice, oppression—in a word, hunger. To pray is to find in my own hunger an echo of the hunger of the world, in my own small cry an echo of the cry for justice that rises like smoke from the scorched earth.

Thy will be done

Prayer is the beginning of wisdom because it is the end of willing. The life of prayer is a slow dying into the will of God, a slow awakening into the freedom of life.

On earth as it is in heaven

Prayer is not a technique of self-improvement. It is not an instrument of spiritual experience. It is beyond all human competency, beyond language and learning and control. Prayer is heaven's speech. To pray is to live beyond the narrow walls of the self and beyond whatever can merely be controlled.

As flowers open to the morning, so the praying life opens towards the will of God, standing up straight into the bright burning presence of the Name.

Give us this day our daily bread

Every day, morning and night, I hunger. The stuff of my life is hunger, need, lack. Affluence and technology might blind me to my need, but a morning without food is enough to show me the truth of what I am. I live by lack; God lives by fullness. I am only hunger; God is only food.

And forgive us our debts as we forgive our debtors

Hurt, disappointment, resentment are always knocking at the door of my life. As soon as I drive one away another starts beating at the door, eager to come in and set up its home in the little house of my heart. I will die of resentment; I am destroyed by what I am owed. But I learn to forgive when God writes off my debts and makes me free. Now I can live, now I can clear the debts of enemies and friends, and speak the magic word of forgiveness that drives resentments back into the dark.

And lead us not into temptation but deliver us from evil

This world is only trial. Yet it is God's world, and all the evils that crowd in upon my life can never hide my voice from the listening God.

For thine is the kingdom, the power and the glory, forever and ever

God is glorious. All my life I was asleep within myself, but when I bowed my head to pray I opened my eyes to the glory of God. Glory ought to be seen. Just as it is right for the ocean to be seen or a piece of music to be heard or the body of a lover to be loved, so it is right to give God thanks and praise, for God is glorious.

Amen

The life of God is prayer itself. It is deep calling to deep, the endless giving and receiving of self-divesting, self-communicating joy. My prayer is an eavesdropping on the Prayer that is God. God's speech is grace and truth, God's life is love, God's silence is the annunciation of the Name. The word of my life is a modest, small, yet glad and true *Amen*.

Arms

My daughter wants to be an artist. Or to be more precise, she *is* an artist. That is the first thing she will tell you about herself, after she has told you her name. From dawn to dusk she can happily do nothing but sit and draw: dozens of pictures, hundreds of them, reams of paper cramming the drawers and cupboards. She will draw us out of house and home. The pictures turn up everywhere. If I pull down an obscure nineteenth-century novel from the shelf, likely as not I'll find a homemade bookmark tucked inside, some improbable picture that she's planted there, hidden away for its day of discovery—or never found at all, it's all the same to her. When I am away, I call her on the phone and she gives me breathless reports on all the day's drawings. She lives for drawing: she breathes in air and breathes out pictures.

Yesterday while I was playing with her at the park, she fell and broke her arm. We didn't get a wink of sleep all night. She lay in bed next to me tossing and turning and commanding me to stroke her arm—"but without *touching* it." She asked for a story, so in the dark I told her a long somnolent tale about a Russian prince who disguised himself as a pauper and went out one winter afternoon to see how all the townsfolk live. He walked from his palace into the hustle and bustle of the town, and no one recognized him. But he wasn't used to the big streets, the mud, the pools of slick ice on the ground, and he slipped in the street and broke his arm. The people rushed to help him. A man in a huge coat took him back to a little house down the lane, and made him lie down while the man's wife tore one of their sheets and bound his arm. She fussed over him and brought him hot stew and a piece of hard stale bread, and begged him to stay the night with them. It was the smallest house the prince had ever seen, smaller than one of the great wardrobes in the palace. It was damp and musty with low ceilings (not a single chandelier), one tiny kitchen window, and a few pieces of plain hard-edged furniture. They made up a bed for the prince beside the kitchen. It was the hardest mattress he had ever known, and the thinnest blanket too. But the fire in the stove was warm and good, and a light snow was falling outside. Before long he had closed his eyes, and he never slept better in his life (broken arm and all). In the morning he went on his way, stepping very gingerly on the icy road. The man and his wife never learned the identity of their guest that night; in fact, they soon forgot all about him. The prince never saw them again either. But as the years passed, from time to time they would wake on a Sunday morning and find—to their never-ceasing puzzlement—that someone had pushed the kitchen window open and slipped something inside. A silver coin, some cheese, a parcel of fine meats, or, once, a single yellow flower, bright and welcoming as sunlight.

When the story was over, there was a long silence. Relieved, I thought she had finally gone to sleep. But then she moved on the bed with a great sob, and said: "But it's my *drawing* arm. I won't be able to draw."

Have you ever broken a limb—as an adult, I mean? In the same situation, you or I would be worrying about the loss of utility: how will I drive? how will I shower? how will I cut my food? But my daughter sees her arm for what it really is: not a useful tool but a boundless aesthetic resource, a limber extension by which shapeless nature and the wilderness of imagination are disciplined into form. The arm is the mind's pencil, the heart's crayon; it is an instrument not of work but of making. One needs it because one needs (every day) to draw the world into being. If you also occasionally use your arm to brush your teeth, then so much the better: it is a happy coincidence, a side effect of the fingers' capacity to grasp a pencil.

Lying in the dark while my daughter wrestled with her thoughts, with that awful bone-cracking discovery of an inhospitable world, I found myself praying. Not just for relief from pain, not just for sleep, but also for her lucid intuition about what her little limbs are for—what *she* is for. May her arm still ache to draw the day the cast comes off. May she never grow satisfied with the tawdry three-dimensional drabness of this world. May she always long to color it, to flatten it into shape, to bring forth those bustling graphite landscapes where the sun bats its eyelashes and all the birds smile knowingly and children's faces stretch out wide from ear to ear, straining to contain the enormous shining bubbles of their eyes.

Berlin

It has been said that great books are the ones that have to teach us how to read them. It is the same with cities. London cannot teach you how to experience New York, any more than Dickens can teach you how to read Dostoevsky. And when you are in Berlin, the correct way to experience the place is by bicycle.

Now there are people—you will have heard of them, I'm sure—who believe that riding a bicycle is a "sport," a way to "keep in shape," something that is merely "good for you." Nothing is more morally or aesthetically objectionable than such a cyclist, zipping through the traffic lights in his skintight lycra suit and shiny torpedo helmet, sanctimoniously sipping water from an aerodynamic flask strapped to his shoulder.

Who is this fellow? What is he about? He is performing that peculiar Calvinistic ritual that is known as Exercise. On the surface he might appear gregarious enough, but in truth he is a mean unsympathetic creature, this secular ascetic with his sculpted buttocks and his strap-on water bottle. He pursues cycling for his own selfish ends, and therefore cannot enjoy it. To him, it is all the same whether the bicycle actually goes anywhere or whether it is fastened to the floor of a gymnasium, a mere simulation, one of those monotonous unmoving Exercise Bikes that are exactly like a real bicycle in every respect except that they have no wheels and cannot propel you down the street.

There are some things that are corrupted by proficiency. The expert lover, the slick preacher, the professional childcare provider—these are not honest things, because good honest preaching and childrearing and lovemaking require some element of awkwardness and ineptitude and surprise, something tenderly human that resists the cold logic of technical mastery. Just so the cyclist: the fast expert sporty cyclist is an ungodly man, you can count on it. He speaks harshly to his children and spends hours grooming his fingernails and has always felt, deep down, that his father didn't love him. He uses the bicycle the way an expert lover uses a woman, his mind absorbed by all the correct techniques for stimulating pleasure, working at her body as coolly and clinically as a pornographer. Such a lover *goes nowhere* with his beloved, just as the Exercise Cyclist goes nowhere on his bicycle but stays imprisoned in his own immaculate body even as he whizzes through the city looking straight ahead with a steely gaze through four-hundred-dollar wraparound pink sunglasses.

Expert cycling, therefore, I abhor. Expert cycling belongs in no proper self-respecting city. But the bicycle as a vehicle—the bicycle not as an instrument of self-improvement but as a machine of transportation, the bicycle as a strictly utilitarian way of getting about town—now *that* is a noble and excellent thing, beautiful and true and good in its rattling clattering swiftness, all legs and arms and wheels and whirling gears.

What could be nobler than a bicycle? For in the bicycle, you take the most marvelous, ancient, portentous triumph of human invention and ingenuity—the wheel!—and append it to the human anatomy so simply, so naturally, that you would think the human body had been designed for nothing else than wobbling about town on a pair of wheels. Perhaps a million years from now the human species will be born with wheels instead of legs; it would be an improvement. But for now, this spoked, sprocketed, handlebarred, rubber-tired, pedal-pushed apparatus supplies what nature lacks.

Berlin reveals itself to the cyclist, just as Paris reveals itself to the walker and Los Angeles to the freeway driver and Dublin to the drinker. If you want to know what Berlin is, throw away your guidebook, forget about all those tourist sites, and don't even *think* about setting foot in one of those brand-new bright red sightseeing buses. If you want to know what Berlin is, all you need is some loose change in your pocket, a scarf around your neck, and a bicycle between your legs.

Blue

The six stained-glass panels of Marc Chagall's America Windows *were presented to the Art Institute of Chicago in 1977, in celebration of the bicentennial of the United States.*

1

For once you decided to avoid religious subjects. You said: I will show the city just as it is—its streets and parks, its art and culture. So you made a city, brought it forth in light and color, and when it was finished you stood back and looked, and what you saw were angels.

2

You saw the city of Chicago as creation. You saw creation aflame with life, alive with music, and all things—from trees and sun to stones and sidewalks—bright and whirling in a whirling dance.

3

Painter of motion and music, you also paint the silences: the book, the desk, the eyes, the little windows. And in the foreground a familiar face, a hand outstretched, five candles burning.

4

They say human society is only power and control. They say it is, at bottom, a stew of blood and violence and old bones. But your windows tell the truth: the world is music, poetry, dance, a book suspended in the sky, a dove beating her wings.

5

People speak of love. But let none say they have loved till they have loved a thing as you loved the color blue. What is blue? Blue is darkness and light, warmth and cold, night and day, inside and outside, earth and sky, singing and silence. Blue is all and in all, the living glow of interior light in every created thing. Blue is the secret fire of creation.

6

On the first day God separated darkness from light, blue from blue.

7

On the second day God separated the waters above from the waters below, blue from blue.

8

If in the beginning God had created nothing but blue, it would have been enough: all the marvelous varieties of that color would sing God's glory, shout God's Name.

9

"There is but one single color that gives meaning to life and art—the color of love" (Chagall).

Books

When I was forced to play team sports as a boy, I would wait in diminishing hope as all the other boys were chosen one by one. In the end there would be two of us left, me and the kid with coke-bottle glasses who couldn't tie his own shoes and who was known to burst into tears if he ever lost the ball or got knocked down. For agonizing seconds the two hairy-legged captains would size us up, until, finally, one would turn to the other and pronounce the cruel verdict: "You can have them." (I cannot lie: this happened even when my own best friend was one of the team captains.)

Yes, I know what it is to be unwanted. I suppose that's why Calvinist theology has always appealed to me, and why I was forever bringing home stray kittens as a boy. It is also why I sympathize with the unwanted book, the book nobody else will buy or read, the book that might have languished in embarrassed silence until the end of the world, unchosen. It is part of Christian belief in the resurrection to assert that nothing is ultimately unwanted, nothing finally lost or forgotten. When the last trump sounds and the sea gives up its dead, whatever was neglected or cast aside will be raised up and kept forever in the presence of the one in whom Memory and Love are joined.

So sometimes when I'm rummaging in the darkest corner of a used bookstore, I will choose a book just because it looks lonely and forgotten. I find myself treating the book with special respect, handling it gently, patiently studying the binding, admiring the typeface, before finally taking it to a special place—a favorite café, or the beach, or the shade of a tree I love—where I can read it slowly and in secret. Like one of those orphaned kittens, I love the book even more because it is rejected by the world. By reading the unwanted book, I give my silent witness to the coming day when all the books will be opened and the last will be first and whatever was forgotten will be remembered in love, world without end.

Boredom

The cultural critic Neil Postman said that we are amusing ourselves to death. Our every waking moment is filled with pleasure, and yet, paradoxically, our lives are afflicted by a strange malaise. Never have we been more entertained; never have we been more bored.

On the whole, Christian theologians have harbored dark thoughts about boredom and have viewed it as a sin. Kierkegaard said that "boredom is the root of all evil," while Jacques Ellul identified boredom—so "gloomy, dull, and joyless"—as a defining perversion of modern social life. Ellul's view was close to that of Karl Barth, who similarly described "the signature of modern human beings" as neither serenity nor rebellion, but simply an "utter weariness and boredom." In Barth's view, "man is bored with himself," and as a result "everything has become a burden to him."

In contrast, the Italian philosopher Giorgo Agamben has offered a more positive assessment of the role of boredom in our lives. Human beings, he says, "cannot be defined by any proper operation," and so our humanness can never be exhausted by any particular task. Agamben speaks of boredom as our "creative semi-indifference to any task." This semi-indifference is linked to a theological truth about human beings: we are not reducible to our work; we will always exceed any given task. Or as Agamben puts it, boredom discloses the essence of a "simply living being." Between our work and our being there lies a gap, and boredom marks that gap (Agamben, *Means without End*).

The gap between being and work is nowhere better depicted than in Andrew Marvell's 1653 poem "Bermudas," which portrays work in a primordial paradise:

> Thus sang they, in the English boat,
> An holy and a cheerful note,
> And all the way, to guide their chime,
> With falling oars they kept the time.

These unfallen human beings are not singing to keep time in their rowing, but rowing to keep time in their song. They are really working, but they exceed their work, and the labor is a needless embellishment, a fitting but unnecessary improvisation. Or to put it more simply, their real work is praise: the rowing of the oars forms the background rhythm of their song. In Agamben's terminology, Marvell's rower could be described as a "being-without-work"—he really works, but his work is superfluous, a celebration rather than a necessity.

But if boredom marks the gap between our being and our work, it also marks the gap between being and enjoyment. At least in the affluent West today, most of us would accept that life cannot finally be boiled down to work. The more sinister threat today is the reduction of life to leisure. A consumer society generates boredom in order to alleviate it. We are always bored, and we are always being rescued from our boredom. As Huxley predicted in *Brave New World*, our society has become one in which there is "no leisure from pleasure." Again, we have closed the gap between being and work, except that now enjoyment has become our true and proper "work."

To face both work and enjoyment with what Agamben calls a "creative semi-indifference" is, today, the gesture of the human being who stands before God and is recognized by God—the human being who is no longer under law (neither the law of work nor the law of enjoyment), but under grace. This human being, this person under grace, is the one whose work and play can never be taken too seriously. They are creative embellishments whose ultimate aim is celebration and praise. Like Marvell's rowers, both work and play find their place only as they serve the modest role of keeping the time in our song:

> And all the way, to guide their chime,
> With falling oars they kept the time.

Breakfast

A prayer with my children

Yours are the bright sun and the blue sky to which we turn our faces as we gather on the lawn. Yours is the smell of steaming pancakes and brewed coffee and fresh-mown grass. Yours is the choreography that sets the wasps in motion while the trees and shrubs applaud.

Felicity has prepared a table for us, and You are the welcome that nearly blinds us as we squint together at the shining plates and glittering knives and forks. You are our fullness as we pile our plates with the pancakes we have made. You are our sweetness as we scoop handfuls of sliced strawberries from the bowl. You are our overflowing bounty, our More Than Enough, as we squeeze the syrup from the bottle, as it oozes and dribbles over everything. You are Anna's generosity when she sees my plate and worries that I will not have enough, when she hands me her own dripping pancake and implores me to receive it. You are the swell of gratitude in James's chest when, overwhelmed by all that breakfast means, he turns and smears my cheek with the kiss of maple-syrup peace.

O grain of the earth and fruit of the strawberry bush! O pancake of joy and syrup of thanksgiving! To You we lift our hearts, and our mouths are full of Your goodness. To You we raise our shining forks and sticky faces, for today heaven and earth are dripping with Your glory. Light of our light, festivity of our feasting, joy of our breakfast picnic: the night's long fast is over, and we give You thanks and praise.

California

The future

"As one went to Europe to see the living past, so one must visit Southern California to observe the future" (Alison Lurie, *The Nowhere City*).

The slide

"In Los Angeles, all the loose objects in the country were collected as if America had been tilted and everything that wasn't tightly screwed down had slid into Southern California" (Saul Bellow, *Seize the Day*).

Pasadena

The night before the Rose Parade, the Oklahoma preacher makes his way down Colorado Boulevard, holding above the crowded sidewalk a big yellow sign about the Bible, the wages of sin, the dreaded afterlife. Ten paces ahead of him, his eleven-year-old daughter keeps the same funereal march, pointing the megaphone straight ahead like a pistol and proclaiming the King James gospel at 120 decibels. I thought: One day she will write a book about all this.

The idea of home

We stayed in a big house on the hill above the sea. Everything was new, clean, polished, straight off the pages of a magazine, migrainously bright. It was not so much a home as the idea of a home, just as Starbucks is the idea of coffee and *The Smurfs 3D* is the idea of a children's movie.

Disneyland

I am a cynic, a hater, a vehement critic of the Disneyfication of childhood. Anyone who will listen, I tell them what's wrong with Disney. I tell them: "You should *not* always follow your heart." I tell them: "The Real You is, at times, an abomination." I tell them: "Your little girl is *not* a princess." I tell the little girls: "Your aim in life is *not* to marry a prince." When we agreed to take our children to Disneyland I made ironic remarks from the corner of my mouth, I spoke of compromises and the sacrifices we make for our children, I prepared myself for the grueling spiritual trials of an entire day at Disneyland, though secretly I wondered whether we might persuade our children to leave a little early. Then the day came. We drove all morning. We walked through the gates and we were in Disneyland. The colored shops and houses were bathed in a soft nostalgic glow, the streets curled away lazily into the distance, a horse-drawn streetcar pulled up beside us, the music of half-forgotten childhood movies played from somewhere beyond the sky. Everything was Sunday and Pollyanna and homemade lemonade and America. I peered carefully at a drifting cloud to check if the sky was real. We stayed for fourteen hours, until my children had to beg me to take them home.

Prison

We were eating breakfast and I was telling him about the evils of the penitentiary system. "You know, the percentage of incarcerated citizens in the United States is seven times higher than in Australia. And a seventh of all those American prisoners—mostly African Americans—are right here in California. It's because the prison systems here operate just like any other corporate enterprise. Did you know that the prison guards union is one of the wealthiest and most powerful political lobbies in California? The Three Strikes legislation, for example—one of the most unjust pieces of legislation in American history—was backed by the prison guards union. For them, it's all about keeping the cells full, expanding the number of prisons, increasing the number of people who work in prisons. A few years back, over 10 percent of the entire state budget was spent on prisons. Just compare that to schools and universities. Compare that to rehabilitation programs. I mean, once you've been incarcerated in California you've got a 90 percent chance of returning to prison—90 percent! My God, do you know how much money is at stake in all this? Do you know how many new prisons have been built in California in the last twenty years? The real dream of these purveyors of human misery is to have half of California behind bars, and the other half gainfully employed as guards in correctional facilities." He chewed his food thoughtfully and said, "Man, I hear you. It ain't easy. Wherever I go, them police move me on. I try to sleep behind the dumpster, they move me on. I stand in front of the store with a cup, they tell me they'll send me back to jail. Man, it *hard* keeping out of jail in California, you got that right."

Los Angeles

He took me hiking in the mountains and in hushed tones told me the names of all the birds. When we had reached the edge of a steep ravine and all we could see were the mountains, the sky, the cool stream and the canyon, he stopped and said, "There it is. My favorite view of Los Angeles."

Whales

The day I went whale watching at Newport, we found ourselves in the middle of a huge pod of killer whales. They swam alongside us and swam in front of us and glided under the boat, their white patches shimmering like immense green lights beneath the water. They were so close, so good and gleaming, so startlingly alive, that it took the greatest effort not to throw myself into the sea in a mad gesture of love and gratitude.

Celebrities

It was a deflating experience. I had gone into Target on the way home because I needed toothpaste, and I stood at the checkout contemplating the infinite melancholy of big department stores. Then in one of the lines I saw a celebrity. Some of the Target staff left their checkouts to go over and shake his hand and tell him that they loved him. I looked down at my tube of toothpaste, averting my eyes, and to tell you the truth I felt very sorry for the poor bastard.

Languages

"I'm going to cycle around Europe," he told me as we started on our second beer. "I dunno, maybe stay and work a while. Maybe learn a language. I've always wanted to learn a language." He had lived all his life in Los Angeles, so I asked him what about Spanish, did he know that Los Angeles has more Spanish-speaking people than any other place in the world, after Mexico City? He said, "Ah, I don't like Spanish, never liked it. It's such a—an *ugly* language." I asked him which languages he liked. "You know, maybe French, Italian, maybe Polish or something like that—hell, I dunno, maybe even German."

Cracks

My son and I were walking down the street and as usual he was carefully stepping over the cracks in the sidewalk. When an old hobo shuffled past in his broken shoes, my son told him matter-of-factly, "If you step on the cracks you'll die." Without stopping the man nodded his grizzled head profoundly and said, "Yeah brother, they hard rules. One false step and it's all over. They hard rules right there, brother."

The mysticism of the freeway

"The freeway experience . . . is the only secular communion Los Angeles has. Mere driving on the freeway is in no way the same as participating in it. Anyone can 'drive' on the freeway, and many people with no vocation for it do, hesitating here and resisting there, losing the rhythm of the lane change, thinking about where they came from and where they are going. Actual participants think only about where they are. Actual participation requires a total surrender, a concentration so intense as to seem a kind of narcosis, a rapture-of-the-freeway. The mind goes clean. The rhythm takes over" (Joan Didion, *The White Album*).

Venice Beach

Along the brokenhearted strip of break dancers, jugglers, graffitied trees, sinister musicians and fortune tellers, amid the slouched storefronts peddling pipes and hotdogs and T-shirts and tattoos, the medical marijuana clinics are newly painted, clean, seedy, legitimate. A guy in dark shades and a bright green lab coat takes a drag on his reefer and sings out, "Step inside, ladies and gentlemen, right this way, the doctor is *in*. Headache, back pain, insomnia, sadness—it's good for whatever ails you."

Australia

I told him I was from Australia. "Australia? For real? It must be nice, all them animals. But you got no sidewalks in Australia—man, that's an amazing place."

Mexico

When I told her I wanted to go to Mexico she said, "Mexico? *Mexico*? What you wanna go there for? Mexico—oh God, it's so gross. You been to Sacramento? You been to *Vegas*?"

Dentist 1

He stumbled into the room, leaning heavily against the wall. His speech was slurred and he had to strain to keep his eyes open when I explained the details of my daughter's accident. She had been running outside with her friends at a Mexican restaurant in Laguna Beach. There was a steel handrail. She didn't see it. She ran right into it. One tooth out. Both front teeth broken. He made me repeat the part about the Mexican restaurant. I explained that we had wanted fish tacos. He slouched out of the room, bumping into the doorframe and murmuring to himself as he wandered off down the hall. It was nine in the morning, and he was either very drunk or (I surmised) had for some years been helping himself to the opiates from the medicine cabinet. Their website boasts that they have their own qualified anesthesiologist; they can provide sedation upon request. When I walked out and told the receptionist that we would not be coming back because the doctor was not sober, she feigned mild surprise—"Really? Not sober?"—and then whispered confidentially, "You could try coming back *tomorrow*."

Dentist 2

Our next dentist was a pretty Iranian woman who pursed her lips sympathetically when my daughter explained how she had broken her teeth. We read the comic books and children's magazines in the waiting room and we got her teeth repaired. She never groaned or flinched, not even once, until it was all over and the dentist gave her a mirror so she could admire her perfect teeth. Only then did she burst into tears, because she had already grown used to those ghastly tomboy fangs. Their jagged edges had become familiar, and she resented her new unblemished American teeth.

Reality

In Balboa Park in San Diego we saw the man with no arms singing country songs and playing guitar with his toes. My son whispered, "Does that man got no arms?" I nodded. He said, "Is he playing with his feet?" I nodded. Then he said doubtfully, "Is that man *real*?" The boy had been to Disneyland, he had been to Malibu, he had seen the film crews at Santa Monica and Altadena. He knew that in California you can never be quite certain whether or not a thing is really real.

Dentist 3

A few days later I heard her telling one of her friends: "When I grow up, I'm going to be a dentist."

Catechesis

The day my mother turned seventeen, she went to the local Canberra police station to apply for a driver's license. When she walked through the door in a short summer dress with a ribbon in her hair, the driving instructor looked up with interest. When she flashed him a smile and said she would like to take the driving test, he thought she was very pretty. When she batted her long lashes and said it was her birthday, he beamed at her and fumbled madly for the police camera, then took her photo and, without further ado, issued her an Australian driver's license. It was, he told her with a sly wink, a birthday present.

And so, without so much as turning a key or operating a windscreen wiper, my mother was authorized to pilot the most dangerous piece of high-speed weaponry ever devised by the crooked mind of man: the automobile.

My mother's older sister had saved up and bought a brand new Mini Minor, the kind all the cool kids were driving in those days. To celebrate my mother's seventeenth birthday, they went on a road trip together to Melbourne. Now the highway from Canberra to Melbourne, if you have never made that journey, is an easy eight-hour drive that takes you through sprawling dairy country, down along the languid Murray River, and up through the hills of the Great Dividing Range. My mother being a licensed driver, her sister gave her a turn at the wheel. On a long, perfectly straight road, without another vehicle in sight, my gleeful mother held the wheel and plunged down her accelerator foot. In the passenger seat beside her, her sister closed her eyes and began to dream. The Mini Minor gathered speed. It began, ever so slightly, to wobble. My mother pushed harder on the accelerator, smiling at the charming dairy fields. When the poor little car began to shake, my mother did as any person driving for the first time might do: she accelerated a little more, and then, to compensate for all that wobbling, began to nudge the wheel from side to side—gently at first, then harder, with a certain jubilant vigor. Side to side, side to side: no doubt about it, it had been a splendid birthday. Dreamily she watched a flock of birds go by. The car was wobbling wildly now. She swerved the wheel harder and felt the accelerator go—at last!—flat to the floor.

That was how it happened that, on a long straight stretch of road, with no vehicles or obstacles of any kind for miles around, the brilliant new hundred-mile-an-hour Mini Minor found itself toppling and rolling like a rugby ball, over and over, until at last it came to rest in a wide ditch, crushed and crumpled, while my mother, breathless with exhilaration beneath a shower of glass confetti, still clasped the wheel with both hands—in fact, still rocked it back and forth with dazed but undiminished glee.

Though they now had no car and little money, the two sisters somehow made their way to Melbourne. A few nights later, at a party in the suburbs, my mother drank wine, talking loudly and laughingly about her marvelous birthday. Then, wandering alone through the house, she noticed some keys on a table and idly picked them up. She twirled the keys around her finger. She went out the front door and twirled them beneath the encouraging winks of the stars. She found the car that fit the key, a lovely red sedan, and climbed into the driver's seat.

It was such a cool clear evening, such a perfect night for driving, my mother thought, as she turned the next corner, windows down and engine blazing. By the time she made it back to the party twenty minutes later, she had reduced her second automobile to a steaming wreck on the corner of a quiet backstreet three blocks away. She brought the keys back, discreetly placed them on the table.

I often think of that good, sweet-natured Canberra policeman who gave my mother her license for a birthday present. On the night of her birthday, I imagine the policeman lounging happily in his favorite chair at home, thinking of the girl with the dimpled smile, congratulating himself on his chivalry, never for a second imagining that he himself was, that night, the most dangerous person in the Commonwealth of Australia. For it was he who had made my mother a Driver, he who had single-handedly turned every other citizen and every vehicle for hundreds of miles into a potential victim of my mother's birthday joy.

In the church today, are we not very much like the innocent-hearted policeman? We would like to make it as easy as possible for people to become Christians. Catechesis is too demanding; education is a bore; disciplined instruction in the Christian faith will only put them off. And so with a knowing wink we waive the requirements and sign the baptism certificate. We are charming, gallant, spiritually magnanimous. In our eagerness to make sure everybody is included, to reassure inquirers that the Christian faith is an easygoing undemanding thing, we are looking only at the dimples and the batted lashes. We forget the longer view, the screech of tires and the shriek of twisted steel and the long split-second when a windscreen becomes a million tiny diamonds in the sky. We even have the nerve to blame new converts if, some time down the road, they make a wreck of their faith.

After considering the matter carefully and objectively, I find I cannot blame my mother for the magnificent trail of automobiles left smoking in her wake: I blame the generous heart of a magnanimous policeman.

Childhood

> The tiny, not the immense,
> Will teach our groping eyes.
>
> —Francis Webb, "Five Days Old"

1

Children ask questions. They appear innocent and naïve, but it is an elaborate ruse. They are involved in the deepest espionage, gathering intelligence and creating profiles on the dangerous foreign country where adults dwell.

2

When I was a little boy my mother took me into town on the bus, and as we came out of a store we happened to meet the Prime Minister. My mother always remembered the day, for we had seen the Prime Minister of Australia; I always remembered the day too, for it was the first time I ever got to ride the bus. Recently at a museum of fashion design, my wife and I were admiring a remarkable dress on a mannequin. Our little boy stood there, awestruck, and said: "But how does she *think* without a head?" The adult has been schooled in desire, and so organizes all perceptions according to an elaborate hierarchy of values. To the extent that the child has not yet learned the discipline of this hierarchy, he is close to the kingdom of heaven. Only the eyes of a child can see that the mannequin is more marvellous than the dress, that it is more wonderful to ride the bus than to meet the Prime Minister.

3

The child has a very limited capacity for Aristotelian abstraction. Seemingly identical slices of cake are not so many species of the genus "slice of cake." To the child, each one is absolutely unique: thus the child wants *this* slice, and will grieve, shaken by sorrow and confusion, if offered an identical substitute. That is the flip side of the child's inherent capacity for wonder: there are no types, no universals, only the particular.

4

The child loves the parent's face. Imagine standing roughly at the level of other people's kneecaps, and you will understand children's almost religious and mystical adoration of the face, their insatiable hunger for direct eye contact with the adult face. The parent who never bends down low to speak with the child is reduced to the role of a mysterious *deus absconditus,* a pair of trousers that occasionally emits abrupt commands from distant heights.

5

The child sleeps. Adults imitate sleep with various degrees of convincingness, but the child really sleeps: in the car, on the floor, in the parent's arms, sitting or lying, while playing and while eating. I have observed a two-year-old standing and resting his head on the seat of a chair, fast asleep on his feet like a horse. I have seen children fall asleep halfway through a mouthful of food, or halfway through a sentence. Children sleep because the world is their bed: a big all-encompassing ontological pillow. That is why so many children have trouble getting to sleep at night. When your existence is permanently enveloped in a commodious cushion, the thought of having to confine yourself to one narrow bed seems vulgar and artificial, like going to the beach and being expected to play in the enclosed sandpit.

6

The child in the womb kicks out towards the heart of the mother. All childhood, compressed like a spring, is contained within this kick. The child loves the mother too much, and pushes away to create room for agency. The parent feels this sudden stab of difference, and sustains it. The parent leans in close so that the child can kick out all the more effectively. The agency of the child and the bruised joy of the parent: they are two sides of the same thing.

7

God is the one "from whom all earthly fathers derive their name" (Ephesians 3:14). The joy and sorrow between parents and children is the echo in time of the Son's sharp kick against the womb of the Father, the sorrow and joy of incarnation.

8

Jesus is the true child. The one who is eternally Child calls God "Parent," and then echoes this call by becoming a human child, by fabricating within our world a child as an exact copy of its eternal form. Human history is an echo of this eternal call and response between Parent and Child.

9

We are children. Not everyone is a parent, but everyone is someone's child. That is the secret of life and the foundation of religion.

Circus

Today my three children underwent one of life's most important rites of passage. An experience that marks a human life forever. A moment that divides each child's life into Before and After. A sacred, solemn, irreversible ritual. A trial of courage and virtue and strength of heart. A transition from the age of innocence to the age of wisdom and understanding and the fear of the Lord.

I am referring, of course, to the circus. For today—I record this so it will never be forgotten—my children went to the circus.

It all started innocently enough. It was a hot day, and they had gone out for ice cream with their grandmother. Driving down the highway, they saw rising in the distance a great tent, high as mountains, bright as sunrise, shimmering beneath billowing flags and golden spires, solitary and immaculate amid a wild debris of cages, cars, and caravans, a giant pinned to the earth by quivering ropes, smiling madly with its cavernous black maw while crowds gathered outside in nervous lines and the one-eyed man by the ticket stand muttered prophecies thick with Russian and rum, casting secretive sideways glances at the wisecracking monkey on his shoulder. That is how, an hour later, my three defenseless children found themselves seated ringside, wide-eyed, beside their grandmother, gripping their seats with joy, as the jugglers hurled knives and the boys swallowed fire and the gymnast danced on the rolling globe and the sparkling trapeze artists flung themselves through space like falling stars.

The circus—that institution of joy, that spectacle of ecumenism, that tent of democracy, that circle of *sobornost*, that festive assemblage of man and beast, sensuality and austerity, laughter and terror, life and death—the circus: is it not one of the last enduring signs of humanity in a world grown bloodless, inhuman, and cold? In a world ruled by the Machine, the circus maintains its raucous witness to the joy of Life. In a world ruled by Work, the circus upholds the true doctrine of the primacy of Play. In a world ruled by Death, the circus proclaims the happy gospel of death's defeat.

It is surely worthy of notice that some of the most imaginative theologians of our time have found particular spiritual solace in the circus. Henri Nouwen likened Christ's followers to clowns—"he who is called to be a minister is called to be a clown." He was spellbound by a German trapeze troupe and followed them from place to place until he had befriended them and they had given him lessons. The trapeze, he said, taught him all he needed to know about the way trust conquers fear. He wrote a book about "clowning" and, in his later years, hoped to write a book on the spirituality of the trapeze—though he never lived to do it.

The lay theologian William Stringfellow had an even deeper obsession with the circus. He compared the circus to the kingdom of God and insisted that the church would be more faithful if it were less like a religious institution and more like a circus. "Biblical people, like circus folk, live typically as sojourners, interrupting time, with few possessions, and in tents, in this world." Like Nouwen, Stringfellow thought the circus exemplified a Christian vision of Christ's triumph over the fear of death. The circus ridicules death, and so becomes a parable of the coming kingdom: "In the circus, humans are represented as freed from consignment to death. There one person walks on a wire fifty feet above the ground, . . . another hangs in the air by the heels, one upholds twelve in a human pyramid, another is shot from a cannon. The circus performer is the image of the eschatological person—emancipated from frailty and inhibition, exhilarant, transcendent over death—neither confined nor conformed by the fear of death anymore. . . . The circus is eschatological parable and social parody" (Stringfellow, *A Simplicity of Faith*). Stringfellow filled his home with circus memorabilia. He subscribed to circus magazines. He spent an entire summer—it was the high point of his life—travelling from town to town with the Clyde Beatty-Cole Brothers Circus, until he had blended imperceptibly with the rest of that caravan of prophets, fools, and dreamers. As a popular itinerant lecturer, he used to plan his speaking schedule around circus routes. When asked how often he attended the circus, he once replied, "Not often. About twenty times a year." Stringfellow always planned to write a full-scale theology of the circus—though, like Nouwen, he died before ever completing that noble piece of intellectual clowning. During a long illness, he built a huge scale model of the Clyde Beatty-Cole Brothers Circus. When he died they played circus music at his funeral.

Think for a moment of the desert fathers and mothers, those ascetics who took to the deserts of Egypt and Syria in the third and fourth centuries. You could make a strong case that the desert ascetics were really a motley crew of wandering circus performers. Half-deranged spiritual clowns dressed in rags, poking fun at worldly wealth and pomp. Ascetic trapeze artists performing their reckless feats atop high columns. Lonely hermits taming the wild beasts as a sign of creation made new. Contemplative acrobats ascending the rungs of their interior ladders while the world looked on, breathless with suspense. Rejoicing clownlike even in sorrow, they renounced the whole wide world as a solemn witness to life and a gigantic joke against death and the devil.

Today as my children swayed in their seats, clutching their hot dogs for dear life, gazing up into the mighty vault of the Big Top while the fearless liturgy spun its circle high above them, I wonder if they heard distant echoes of another performance, another time and place where weary souls drag themselves in from the dust and heat and huddle in a circle, scared and hopeful, hardly believing their eyes when a clownish figure lifts bread and wine like a juggler and bellows out the great joke that is the exhilarating, momentous, stupendously funny secret at the center of the universe: "Christ is risen!"

Icon of the Holy Cross. Painted by Deacon Matthew D. Garrett; used by kind permission of the artist.

Cross

On the icon of the Holy Cross

1

The icon depicts revelation: the crucifixion of the human Jesus as the appearance of the eternal God. The divine being is eternally cross-shaped, even as it is eternally radiant.

2

The crucifixion of Christ is the secret of eternity, the true and only glory that shines forever from the abyss.

3

At the center of Christian devotion is not a revealed doctrine, a religious ideal, or even a right way of life, but an embodied human person. Christianity began not with beliefs about Jesus, but with people who had *known* Jesus. They were affected by Jesus as one is affected by friendship, not as one is affected by reading a powerful book or encountering a new idea. "That which was from the beginning, which we have heard, which we have seen with our eyes, which we have looked upon, and our hands have handled" (1 John 1:1). The heartbeat of Christian faith is a fact as tangible as wood and nails.

4

The crucifixion is depicted here as realistically as is possible within the bounds of iconography. The human Jesus stretches out his arms across a rough-hewn wooden beam. His body is bent, his feet twisted, his hands pierced, his head turned down in sorrow.

5

Around the earthly historical cross shines an eternal heavenly cross. This budded cross is clean, unbloodied, perfect; its form is untouched by the harsh lines and distorted perspectives of the small internal cross. Its form is light itself, the glory of eternity. Everything contingent, historical, earthly is suspended amid this timeless light, absorbed into the serene balance of perfect form. The budded cross is the true essential form, the Platonic reality, that projects the earthly crucifixion like a black shadow on the wall of the cave of time.

6

The eternal cross is a theodicy. Death and hell are safely circumscribed within its shining frame.

7

At the top of the icon, the divine face of Christ peers through the curtains, high above the earthly historical cross of Jesus. Unlike the face of the crucified one, this Christ-face looks straight ahead, reminding us that its own impassive glory is the hidden truth of the crucifixion. On either side, the saints gather reassuringly, springing like flowers from the barren wood. They model for us our own proper response to the spectacle of the crucified one. We are to respond with adoring humility and reverent submission. The presence of the saints makes the cross safe, familiar, accessible. There is, the icon assures us, a proper human posture that corresponds to the fact of the cross. The cross stands not merely over and against us but alongside us, in uninterrupted continuity with our religious piety.

8

Is not history—the history of Jesus—completely fixed and immobilized in this representation? Is it not suspended in eternity like a beautiful figure in a glass ball?

9

Are we not left with the impression that the icon is wholly right in what it shows, yet somehow also wholly wrong? Its sole aim is to set forth Christ as the truth of eternity, the truth that shines forever, the truth of God. But in the very act of showing this, the icon allows the impassive majesty of eternal truth to eclipse the brute fact of the cross of history.

10

When I was a boy, I lived in a vast sprawling mansion beside the sea on a tropical island in North Queensland. When I had grown up, I went back one day to the island and saw my childhood home: a tiny dilapidated fibro shack with a tin roof and cracked concrete floors, scarcely more than a backyard shed. All my life, the real earthly house had been eclipsed by the fantasy house that my memory had built for me as, year after year, I silently venerated my childhood. The fantasy house was beautiful: but it was fantasy.

11

As though we cannot venerate Christ without immediately turning him into an idol, an eternal idea instead of an embodied fact. As though religious piety produces an immediate and inevitable transformation of the cross into a smooth, well-balanced object, something easily grasped and held in the hand, an instrument not of judgment but of consolation.

12

Theological truth and spiritual fantasy are thus bound together in the icon, as close as wheat and tares or light and day.

13

You can see why Karl Barth so loved Grünewald's terrible painting of the crucifixion. In Grünewald, one finds a complete repudiation of Christian Platonism: a theology of the cross stripped bare of glory. Yet Grünewald's Protestant aesthetic has its own perils. Without something like a Platonic anchoring, are we not right on the brink of a steep descent into theological nihilism? In beholding the earthly historical cross devoid of all religious mediation, do we not find ourselves at the doorstep of hell?

14

Or is that, perhaps, where we are meant to find ourselves when we contemplate the cross?

15

The truth of the icon—a truth that Grünewald all but obliterates—is that there is, for us, no means of access to Christ except through religious veneration. Our only contact with Christ is through worship in the company of the living tradition of the saints—even if worship immediately becomes indistinguishable from idolatry. We cannot have Christ without religion: that is the truth that the icon teaches. But—this is what the icon forgets—we can speak of "true religion" only as we speak of a "justified sinner" (Karl Barth).

Curls

There was once a man whose scalp was blighted by an appalling shock of red curls. He had suffered from this condition ever since the nurses had poked their heads over the edge of his crib beneath the glaring lights, tickling his tummy and saying, "My oh my, would you just look at that hair!" His mother dressed him in an array of hideous orange costumes while he blew bubbles of spittle and flailed his arms in protest (he tried to undo the buttons and remove the clothes, but could never quite keep his infant hands steady: trying to control them was like chasing a pair of rabbits), and all the neighbours came by to say, "Well halloo dair liddle bubbyboy, oooh aren't your wittle curls so adowable, awww and lookit your bootiful wittle itty-bitty owange outfit, ooh wittle schmoochie-poochie-poo, oh so pwetty, ooh yes, coochie-coochie-coochie-coo."

He was disgusted by the attentions of these women, the slobbery humiliations of their lipsticked advances, their plump bejewelled fingers jabbing at his ribcage, their wobbling jowls looming over him like a German airship, and their rambling rhapsodic homilies about his hair. He tried to ward them off, waving his arms furiously, but that only seemed to draw them like flies to a honey pot. He tried to frighten them away, howling and screaming and kicking like a mule, but then they redoubled their efforts, stroking and cajoling him, or even scooping him up and flinging him over the vertiginous heights of their shoulders, or squashing him against their intolerable dry breasts while they sighed and crooned, wobbling about in the throes of a terrible and ludicrous dance.

But he was a kind-hearted fellow, even at that age, and he never once blamed all this on the incorrigible women, or on his unfaithful mother who had let them into the house. No, he laid the blame right where it belonged: on that abomination of curls that perched upon his head, turning his pale face into a gleaming beacon, a round white road sign circled in red.

When he was five years old, the pretty little French girl and her ugly French parents moved in next door. He was madly, fiercely in love with her for exactly three minutes, from the moment she stepped out of the car into the sunlight, licking a strawberry paddle pop like a cat, until she walked over to him, brushed back the neat fringe from her startling green eyes, and said, "Bonjour, how do you do, you must be my new neighbor, my name's Juliette, I'm from Paris, that's in France, do you like my new dress, I like your hair, what's your name, are you a boy or a girl?" By the time the first few words had escaped her lips, he knew he was happier than he had ever been in his life; by the time she pronounced the lovely syllables of her name, he was contemplating marriage and wondering how many children they would have; by the end of her speech, he hated her more than anyone he'd ever known, and instead of answering her impertinent question he screwed his face up like a ghoul, stuck out an angry pink tongue, gave her a good hard shove, and wiped his hand on the side of his pants, saying, "Eeeeew, girls' germs," before scampering back inside like a frightened possum.

No, he never was much of a ladies' man, a fact that is hard to account for unless we put it down to that slithering snake pit upon his brow.

As far as hairdressing goes, his mother lacked the tools, the training, the experience, the eye for detail, and the even temper to ever really distinguish herself in that field. But she had a wooden stool, a pair of scissors, and a comb, and so, two or three times a year, she would take him out to the backyard and sit him down to cut his hair. To say he had mixed feelings about these episodes would be euphemistic. It is true that he had longed for nothing more than this, every day craving it, ever since those first malignant red squiggles had reasserted themselves above his ears. It is also true that there was nothing he dreaded more. For his own lifelong inability to sit still in one place for more than eight consecutive seconds produced catastrophic results when you combined it with his mother's lifelong inability to tolerate anything that moans, mumbles, whines, whinges, and generally wriggles about as restless as a worm on a hook.

At the start of the Haircut—before everything escalated into the usual hurricane of snot and tears and murderous threats—he would plead with her, demanding that she cut off all the curls. "But I love your curls," she would say. "Cut them off!" he would say. Oh how he longed for the soothing oblivion of baldness, the blithe anonymity of the short-back-and-sides! When it was all over, he would stand in the bathroom with the tap running, pretending to be brushing his teeth while he patiently scrutinized the shape of his head in the mirror, turning from side to side in a painstaking and meticulous inspection, examining it from every angle to ensure that every last obnoxious question mark had been eradicated.

He never learned much at school, since he was always preoccupied with more important things. During math he drew cockatoos and clowns and dingoes in the cover of his book. During history he sketched designs for fighter planes and steam trains and spacecraft. During science (his favorite subject) he drew a tree, a fence, a rainwater tank, a windmill, the ruins of a farmhouse, and a pair of kangaroos standing on a dirt road. During English he held his pocket knife in his lap and whittled his pencils into little sculpted figurines, or etched trains and cars on the brittle timber underbelly of the desk. At lunchtime he could be seen eating his Vegemite sandwich or kicking a soccer ball or playing marbles or glancing furtively at his reflection in an empty window and smoothing down the hair above his ears with moistened fingers.

One day when he was twelve years old, there was one of those school sports days when all the swaggering boys scramble to outdo each other in the winner-takes-all race towards manhood—grunting, cursing, spitting, kicking dust, picking scabs, assembling in solemn huddles to compare the hairs on their legs and the shoes on their feet, hotly debating the secrets of semen and cigarettes, exchanging heroic autobiographical tales of sex and violence, determining which of the girls were shaving their legs, which of the girls were shaving their armpits, which of the girls were wearing bras. Then all of a sudden Mrs. Nickles, the tuckshop lady, lurched over to where he stood amid the scrum of murmuring boys, ruffled his hair with her greasy tuckshop fingers, grimacing gleefully with her ghastly gold-toothed smile, and said (while all the boys sniggered behind their hands), "Such pretty curls darlin, such a pity you're not a girl."

The next morning he stole five dollars from his mother's purse, wagged school, and walked in drizzling rain to the barber shop, where he had his hair clipped short, as straight as knives.

Time passed, and somehow or other he pieced together a life for himself. He married a girl who worked at the bakery but dreamed all her life of working at the library; she wore blue-rimmed glasses, read the same six novels over and over, and knew the whole three hours of *The Sound of Music* by heart. The first time they made love, her skin smelt of bread and cinnamon; she draped her strapless floral dress over the chair and pulled him down on to the floor, and afterwards she ran her fingers through his hair, though he never knew it because by then he was asleep. Over time they acquired a house, a car, a black-and-white television with rabbit-ear antennas, a bed that her parents had given them, a garden that was always dying but never quite dead, a dog that dug up the garden and chewed up the bed, two cats that were hardly ever seen, and a son who scampered around the house beneath a tangled mop of luxuriant red curls.

On weekdays he wore a wide-brimmed cotton hat to work, and did not take it off again until he came through the front door at six o'clock. When he was not working, he assembled jigsaw puzzles and made leather bags and built his own transistor radio and subscribed to magazines about model trains. He replaced the back screen door, fixed up the bathroom, made wardrobes and bathroom cupboards, replaced the kitchen bench and the wiring in the oven, and built a little shelf beneath the bedroom window for his wife's six novels. For his son, he built three wooden trains, six wooden puzzles (one of them so large and elaborate that it was never fully assembled), a castle with an opening portcullis and drawbridge, a jack-in-the-box with the painted face of a clown, two clown string puppets, a bed in the shape of a racing car with a movable door and leather pouches underneath for toys, a toolbox with sliding drawers and many small compartments, an abacus, a spinning top, a drum, a fire truck painted red with an electric flashing light, a tiny balsa wood yacht with a plastic sail and cotton rigging, and, out in the backyard beside the shed, a two-room cubbyhouse with miniature furniture, a miniature transistor radio, a bookcase, a secret trapdoor in the kitchen floor, and a front veranda with little wooden deck chairs.

That is how he spent his weekends in the big garden shed, hammering and painting and sewing and stitching, while the boy looked on in silence or asked questions or scuttled around the floor scooping up bent nails and woodshavings and globs of dried glue that sometimes got caught in his hair.

Then one hot December afternoon he grew tired of the wooden pirate finger puppets that he was making. He grew tired of *The Sound of Music*. He shouted at the boy and slammed a door. He took up smoking. He began to work late. The wooden pirate finger puppets languished unfinished on the workbench in the shed.

That was when he began to forget things.

Here are the things he forgot. He forgot to fix the bathroom tap, which dripped for four months and three days. He forgot to fix the kitchen screen, and the flies and mosquitoes moved into the house. He went to the store for bread and milk but came back with tinned peaches, or paper cups, or Swiss cheese, or insect spray, or tubes of toothpaste, or mosquito coils, or pickled onions, or plum jam, but no bread and no milk. He forgot to treat the dog for fleas, and he could hear the melancholy scratching in the night. He forgot why he had ever loved his wife, and she grew restless and dejected. He forgot to renew his magazine subscriptions, and finally forgot that he had ever loved the model trains with their tiny clockwork engines and their lovingly weathered landscapes.

There was also the time, one Saturday afternoon, when he tied his shoelaces and put on his hat and climbed on to the roof to clean the leaves from the gutters, and forgot to come down again for his two o'clock appointment at the barber. He forgot all the next day as well, and all the next week, and all the week after that.

Then one morning as he was rubbing his eyes and yawning and walking to the kitchen, he caught a sudden sideways glimpse of himself in the hallway mirror. He stopped. He leaned forward. He narrowed his eyes. He stared intently at the clusters of shy red ringlets springing out above his ears. He turned his head to one side, then the other, then back again. He walked into the kitchen, hands on hips, and stooped down to the place where his son sat playing with a painted wooden train. He frowned silently, his brow creased in concentration as he scrutinized the boy with the round freckled face, the pink ears, and the frightful mess of curls. Then he went back to the mirror and looked again, frowning deeply.

And then, all at once, he remembered all the things he had forgotten.

Daylight fell slanting through the blinds across the floor as he marched back into the kitchen. He had never noticed it before, how much like his son he looked. There was no denying it: he was the spitting image of the boy.

He went out through the backdoor barefoot across the grass towards the garden shed. The grass was cool and wet beneath his feet. He stopped to wait for the boy to catch up, sunlit red mop bouncing as he ran. In the darkness of the shed, the half-made pirate finger puppets lay waiting. He hitched up his pants a little, rocked back on his heels a little, raised his hand and ran five fingers through his hair. Somewhere in the trees a bird had started singing. He looked down at his son. He felt, for the first time in his life, rather dashing.

Drawing

My daughter saw an animated film about a girl and a witch, and she was very frightened. Every night after that she saw the face of the witch, cruel and terrible, in her dreams. She wept for horror, because the witch had turned her nights into a prison, her soft white bed into a dungeon. I told her I would cure her of the nightmares. I found a picture of the witch's face, and at the kitchen table we sat down with pencils, with paper, and with the picture of the witch. She drew the face, and drew it again until she had learned to draw it from memory. Then she understood her terror, that it came only from techniques of line and shadow, from the shape of the eyes, the direction of the eyebrows, the proportion of the mouth, the subtle curling at the corner of the lips, the unnatural length of the fingers, the way the long black cloak enfolds the body and conceals it like a secret. Then the nightmares stopped; then the witch's face no longer leered out from the darkness of her dreams; then her bedroom walls no longer echoed with cruel laughter when the lights went out. But some time later she came into our bedroom as before, creeping up between us in the middle of the night, burying her face in my neck because she was afraid, because her fears had folded over like a cloak, because in her bed she had dreamt the hand of a witch clutching a crooked pencil, scratching white lines on a black page, patiently bringing to life a face, her face, the frightened face of a frightened child.

Virgin of Vladmir Icon. Image courtesy of St. Isaac of Syria Skete.

Face

On the icon of the Virgin of Vladimir

1

Behold the handmaid of the Lord!

2

There are paintings you can look at for a time and be done with them. The Virgin of Vladimir is not that kind of picture. You could look at it all your life, and you'd still just be getting started—or rather, you'd be getting even further away from sounding out its depths. To look at an icon is to "fast with the eyes" (Dorotheos of Gaza).

3

Though the face of the Virgin at first absorbs all our attention, the insistent face of the child is, in fact, older and wiser and more—how else to put it?—more *eternal*. The small face constitutes the real center of the icon and the real source of its radiance. Reflecting his light, the Virgin shines. Her infinitely sad, infinitely strong face is pulled towards the commanding gravity of this center.

Yet observe the child's face, turned upwards and pressed so eagerly against the face of the mother. Look at his expression. Is it not something strangely akin to—worship? If I met someone who did not know what it meant to worship, I could hardly do better than to point to this picture, to this child's face, and say, It looks like that.

On the one hand, there is a real religious danger here: the danger of allowing Christ's mother to become an independent center of religious devotion. But on the other hand, there is something right and true in characterizing this child's relation to his mother as a kind of "worship." For no other word comes close to conveying the extent of Christ's devotion to humankind. His single-minded preoccupation with humanity is a kind of madness, a lucid intoxication. To unworthy humanity he ascribes all imaginable worth. As though he valued us—literally, worshipped us—above all other things, even his own life, even the life of God.

4

The disturbing political and ideological role of the Virgin of Vladimir in Russian history is completely bound up with what is so pure and so instructive in it: namely, its veneration of the bond between this Child and this Mother. Look at the mother's invincibly tender clasping of her son, and you will understand the Russian people's conviction of an absolute and unbreakable bond to the sacred motherland. For the Vladimir icon is a representation not only of Christ and the Virgin but also of a transcendent bond between the Russian people and their Mother Russia.

It is this that makes it possible to comprehend the otherwise quite bewildering way that "Russia" routinely appears in Orthodox theological writing not only as a legitimate contextual concern but as a proper doctrinal topic in its own right. The iconographer was, of course, reflecting this preexisting habit of mind, this tendency to elevate Russian belonging to a transcendent status; but it must still be said that the Vladimir icon—the most venerated image in all of Russia—has burned that conviction on to the Russian imagination for nearly a thousand years. You need only look at the icon to understand why nationalistic sentiment is so closely bound up with the hidden core of Russian religious life; why the history of modern Russian thought is essentially the story of the Slavophiles; and why, for non-Slavic Christians, a thoroughgoing conversion to Russian Orthodoxy proves all but impossible.

5

The theological intuition underlying the whole tradition of Russian iconography is that there are, really and essentially, only two human faces: the face of Christ, and the face of his Mother. All other human persons have their own peculiar distinctiveness, their own particular faces, to the extent that they participate in these forms. For the Orthodox, it is not Adam and Eve who are the prototypes of humanity, but the New Adam and the New Eve—so that the fundamental human relationship is not that of man and woman (Karl Barth) or of husband and wife (John Paul II), but of child and mother. The single form of Virgin and Child is the prototype of every human form: "The divine image in humankind is disclosed and realized as the image of two: of Christ and of his Mother" (Sergei Bulgakov).

6

The truth of this came home to me as I was writing these lines the other night. My wife and children were away for the weekend, so I had gone out alone to a jazz bar to hear some music and do a bit of writing. It was approaching midnight, and I was drinking scotch and scratching with my fountain pen in a crumpled notebook, with a postcard-sized copy of the Vladimir icon propped up on the table in front of me. A pretty girl came over and wanted to know what I was writing. "Let me guess, a music reviewer," she said. But I had to admit that I was writing about a twelfth-century religious painting. She asked about the picture and listened to my explanation with keen interest. Then she leaned close to me—quite close—and began to seduce me. I was flattered, but also saddened as I looked into the sad eyes of the Virgin of Vladimir. As though the human person could become an instrument of promiscuity—something freely offered to a stranger in a bar—only by a careless defacement of Her face, Her holy form. "Her face is beautiful," said the girl in the bar as she peered through the haze at the icon on the table, casually brushing my arm. "Like a sculpture."

When she said that, I loved her and saw that her own face, too, was lovely as a work of art. So I blessed her with my eyes and walked out in the rain and went home, alone, thinking of how the lines of the girl's face had seemed—just for a second, beneath the smoke and shadows and dim lights—like a lovely, sad quotation of the holy face of the Virgin, radiant though fallen.

7

"There is only one face in the whole world that is absolutely beautiful: the face of Christ" (Dostoevsky).

Feast

A true story

Beneath the blue skies of Switzerland, in the bustling town of Basel, there once lived a great theologian. Each week he taught a seminar at the university, ruminating and chewing his pipe while students crowded the floor, pressed hard against the ancient walls, laughing at his jokes and answering his questions with nervous sincerity. He spent his evenings drinking wine and going to concerts and entertaining visitors from faraway places who asked him questions shyly in halting German. On weekends he threw bread to the ducks at the river or rode horses or went to see the animals at the zoo. On Sunday mornings he went to prison and preached in the whitewashed chapel; he spoke like a young man (though he was old, with a heart full of old men's stories), and after the service he exchanged cigars and jokes with the inmates, assuring them that God was, after all, a very happy God.

But more than anything, the theologian loved to return each day to his study. At his desk he was a dark little question mark hunched in a crumpled suit amid curling pipe smoke and walls of books that peered down at his labors with the curiosity of indulgent friends or obstinate relatives. In this manner, day in, day out, he filled reams of paper with that cramped inky hand of his. Volume upon volume tumbled brick-like from the press, solemn great tomes as big and hard as workmen's boots.

And so it was that, as he sat thus smoking and writing, the fame of his books spread far and wide. Throughout Europe and in remote places—South Africa, Scotland, America, Japan, Australia—people discussed his books at dinner parties, held conferences about his ideas, wrote books and then entire libraries about his thoughts. The Holy Father sought an audience with him. Martin Luther King wrote about him. The Japanese formed a school around his name. The Catholics invited him to their council. The Americans splashed his face across the cover of *Time* magazine. His birthdays were greeted with a clamor of praise, while printing presses in many languages ground out books and journals and essays to honor or refute him. His followers proclaimed his heavy tomes to be the dawning of a new era, while some antagonists and former students devoted every waking hour to trying to prove him wrong on even one small point. Whole scholarly careers were busily occupied in this fashion.

The theologian was bemused by these attentions. He enjoyed it all in his own self-deprecating way. And though he travelled and shook hands and talked gravely and accepted honorary degrees, always he returned before long to that little desk with its pipe and pen and tantalizingly clean sheets of paper—empty slates shimmering with promise, like the formless matter in the beginning beneath those gentle brooding wings.

Then one December night, while the snow slept on the ground and all the city's children lay dreaming of Christmas, the theologian died.

Quite suddenly he awoke and found himself standing at the gates of heaven. An angel took him by the elbow and led him in, explaining in hushed tones that everyone was waiting. Inside the gate, the city was bustling with sound and color, like Basel's Market Square in the summertime. The theologian looked around. He tried to take it all in. Then somewhere in the crowd a voice announced his name, and there followed a great cheer. Women and men pressed in close, clasping his hands and thumping his back warmly. Children laughed and clapped their hands. Angels blushed and fluttered their wings in the sunlight.

The theologian felt quite overwhelmed by the crush of bodies, the vigorous handshakes, the beaming faces. He tried to smile and nod politely, as he had always done when receiving a foreign dignitary or an honorary doctorate. He was relieved when again the angel took him by the elbow and steered him through the crowd, out to a side street off the busy square.

They walked on a little way. The theologian, still trying to regain his composure, confessed that he hadn't expected quite so warm a reception. Surprised, the angel assured him that everyone in the city knew his name and they had all been expecting him.

"For are you not Karl Barth?" the angel declaimed with a theatrical flourish. "Of *course* we have heard of the great Karl Barth!" The theologian nodded modestly, as he always did when someone spoke this way, and the angel continued: "Aren't you the one who visited the prisoners on Sundays? Didn't you eat and drink with them? Didn't you tell them jokes to make their hearts glad? Didn't you put cigars in their mouths and hold the match for them? Didn't you go to see them when even their own families had forgotten them? Why my dear fellow, there is not a person in this city who doesn't know your name!"

The theologian stopped in the street. He looked at the angel. "The prison? Well, yes, I see. But all this celebration. I thought perhaps—my theology. My books."

"Ah!" the smiling angel said, and touched his arm reassuringly. "There's no need to worry about all that! It's all forgiven now."

"Forgiven?" said the theologian.

"But of course! In this place, all the books are forgiven—every last word!" The angel took his hand. "No need to dwell on all that now—everything is forgiven here. Come now, my dear, there are still so many people waiting to meet you. And the prisoners you visited—they live down there by the river, in the finest part of town—they've prepared a feast to welcome you. Just wait till you see what a real feast looks like! Come along now, come along."

And so, hand in hand beneath the summer sky, the angel and the theologian made their way together down the city street.

Forgiven

So it has come to this. I am going to die. I wish I could tell you otherwise. I wish I had something more positive to say. For a long time things were fine. I reassured myself: I will not die. I reassured others, not so much by what I said as by my general demeanor. Don't worry, I always seemed to be telling them, nothing to be alarmed about, I will not die.

I have been thinking about this since I was a few years old, only a boy. A woman who'd drifted into our home and moved in with us, a real brokenhearted bundle of nerves, ran over her cat one day in the driveway. The cat died. It lay there and wouldn't get up. It wouldn't play or drink milk or anything. It was dead.

My father explained it to me. He was delicate, careful with his words, almost apologetic when he explained it. Everything dies, that's what he told me. He spread his hands in a gesture of helplessness. I could see the embarrassment in his face, as if this whole unseemly business of dying and being dead were somehow his fault. Forgive me, he seemed to be saying, the cat has died because all things die; forgive me.

After he had explained it to me, I gave it a great deal of consideration. I was evenhanded about the matter, I weighed up the pros and cons as fairly as I could, but in the end I decided this sort of thing just isn't for me. Dying—it's fine for cats, it's fine for other people (strangers especially), but it's not the kind of thing for me.

So I decided I would not die.

Of course there is a lot to be said for dying, I know that. Think of the alternative. Consider the indignity of watching your children and your children's children entering the slow decline of a second infancy. Think of the endlessness of old age; the terrible strain on a diminishing circle of perpetual carers; the constant expansion of aged care facilities, until finally entire cities would be nothing more than gigantic understaffed nursing homes, crowded with the ghostly figures of those who have lived forever but have forgotten their lives and even their names. Or even worse, imagine living forever without ever forgetting, tormented by regret for everything you ever said and did, so that everything hurts more acutely with every passing year, world without end.

Living forever is not all it's cracked up to be—even as a boy I could see that. In the long run, it makes a great deal of sense for other people to die, for everyone to die. I wasn't naïve. I reconciled myself to the fact of death. Yet pondering all this at the age of three or four as I looked into the eyes of the small dead cat, I thought the universe ought to make an exception in my case.

And yet here I am, dying after all. How did it ever come to this?

I went to see a doctor and he gave it to me straight. It's my heart, that's what he told me. Apparently I have a condition that makes my heart wear out after the first seven or eight decades of my life. Subtract from that a few years for every unhealthy lifestyle choice I've ever made along the way: smoking, drinking, not jogging, using butter instead of margarine, too much salt, too much sugar, too much of the wrong sort of fat, not enough of the right sort of fat, too many of the wrong kinds of drugs, not enough of the right kinds, too much sitting in front of the television, not enough rest, not enough vegetables, too many non-organic vegetables with all those nasty carcinogens sprayed all over them, all subtracting year after year after year from an already perilously short life. Taking everything together, I'll be lucky if I get another forty years out of this heart. Less than thirty if my grandfathers' lousy tickers are anything to go by. Bloody genes, can't live with them, can't live without them.

If I knew what was good for me I'd be running around the block right now or lining up for a gym membership instead of squandering my remaining time sitting in a chair (subtract 4 years) having coffee (subtract 1.5) and a butter croissant (subtract 2) and writing down these dying words.

What should I tell you? What can I say for myself? What message should I leave you from beyond the grave? That I should have used margarine after all? That organic veggies are really worth the extra expense, once you factor death into the equation? Or maybe something more personal: "Dad, you were right about death. I forgive you." How would that sound?

No, death and dying notwithstanding, I guess all I'd really like to say is that I'm glad to have been alive. That alive is a very good thing to be, and I have not a single word to say against it. That I have loved songs and eating and drinking and morning and evening and the way friends' voices sound around a campfire in the dead of night. That I have loved animals, especially dogs and cats, and if I had ever got to know horses properly I would have loved them too. That I have seen whales, have witnessed their rolling bigness, and have loved them very much. That I have loved books and reading, have loved rereading books and remembering what it was like to read them for the first time. That I have loved the sound of a pen scratching on paper in a silent room. That I have loved the faces of my friends (I hope somebody will remember all those faces after I'm gone). That I have loved strangers' faces too, old men and old women and beautiful women whose faces I fell in love with and never forgot even though I only saw them once, across a crowded room or in a train or on a bridge as I walked by. That I have loved my wife's face and my wife's words and my wife's skin and the way my wife thinks when she is happy or when she is sad or when she is tired or first wakes up, wide awake and hatching plans while I am still trying to dream. That I have loved my—

My children.

As I sit here now, as I sit dying, my heart slowly wearing out inside me, that is all I really want to tell you. I have loved all of it and I don't have a word to say against it. To tell you the truth, I even love the things that I have hated. Doing wrong, being wronged, this whole miserable business of hurt and misunderstanding and mistakes. I have loved all that because I have loved forgiving and being forgiven. Yes, that's what I have loved most of all. If I could do it all over again I would make all the same mistakes and let all the same mistakes happen to me too, if it only meant that I could have the chance, just once, to forgive, to be forgiven.

Life is very wonderful, and the meaning of it all is the forgiveness of sins, that's what I'd like to tell you. I am glad to have learned that. I am glad to have been alive and to have made so many mistakes and to have borne the brunt of so many too. It is wonderful, all of it.

It is thirty years since the day my father explained death to me, since I looked into the wise dead eyes of the cat and understood. I'm trying, but I still haven't reconciled myself to dying, not really. But when that faulty clock inside me stops ticking and there is no one about to wind it up again, I hope I will be able to die just as I have lived: forgiven.

German

I was brought up proper. So I know that, in conversation, you should always interrupt the other person halfway through their sentence. It is how you show you're really interested. Speaking is the most enthusiastic form of listening. If your conversation partner says something you like, something you agree with, something you find exciting or important or objectionable or even mildly fascinating, all at once you must sweep into action with a sentence of your own. And if all goes well, you will never have to finish that sentence, because the other person will reciprocate with another good interruption.

Every conversation is a minefield. The things that interest me lie buried beneath the surface, waiting to detonate as soon as they are touched. The moment you trigger my interest in what you're saying, you can be sure your own sentences will be blown to smithereens. And, in turn, if I have said something interesting and worthwhile, I naturally expect my sentences to be left unfinished too. Why finish a sentence—finishing things is such a bore—when there is someone else around to start a new one?

And so the whole conversation is carried not by even turns but by a series of abrupt lurches and collisions. If nobody does me the courtesy of interrupting me, my own words have a tendency to trail off inconsequentially. Without being interrupted at just the right moment, I lose interest in my own sentences and cannot be bothered trying to finish them.

Such conversation is less like tennis than like a game of rugby. Not an orderly to-and-fro, but a wild haphazard flinging back and forth, punctuated by an occasional mad dash or brutal tackle or, if the ball is dropped, a quick ungainly struggle of seizing and grabbing, limbs flailing. That is how I expect any ordinary conversation to unfold.

If my wife is angry with me and wants to torment me, she only has to practice what is called "active listening": a horrible, insulting procedure whereby the listener nods, raises eyebrows, makes encouraging indistinct noises while you are speaking—instead of the proper thing, which is to contradict, expostulate, ridicule, vociferate, interject. When I am giving a lecture to my students, I get restless and deflated if fifteen minutes passes without some disturbance. It is a sign that I have failed to engage them; if they were really interested in what I had to say, they would all be talking over the top of me. Polite, silent, attentive, "active" listening is intolerable: it depresses me the way some people are depressed by cursing, shouting, thumping on tables. *Hyperactive* listening is the only kind I like.

Which brings me to that difficult and delicate subject: the German sentence. For all its elegant clockwork precision, for all its gothic poetical homeliness, the disadvantage of the German language is that it cannot be interrupted. For if you interrupt a German sentence halfway through, you will never get to learn what the verb was—whether she agrees to marry you or doesn't; whether their house was saved or destroyed in the fire; whether the person who invited you to dinner is horrified by cannibalism or is an eager practitioner. With the verb coming at the end of the sentence, and with the ever-present possibility that even the most opinionated sentence might end with that astounding little word *nicht*, interruption is, for all practical purposes, impossible. There is nothing else for it. You are in for the long haul. You will have to speak in entire sentences and, what's worse, listen to them too.

Presumably that is where the impressive seriousness of German scholarly discourse comes from: from the habit of listening to a person all the way to the end of the sentence. Academic conferences in English know no such foreign niceties. For us, a gathering of scholars is judged not by who can speak and listen the best, but by who can provide the most brilliant interruptions. "I have heard your subject, I have heard your verb, now let me tell you, sir, what *I* think!" This is excellent, and it is why our conferences are, as a rule, much more entertaining than the ones in Germany.

You can see the whole difference between these two languages if you walk into a Berlin bar around midnight. At any respectable English establishment at that hour, everyone is talking, all together, all at the same time, all constantly and without ceasing. It is not so much a con-versation as a pan-versation. But at your cozy Berlin bar, you find people gathered respectfully in little huddles, speaking and listening in earnest, one voice at a time, everyone taking turns as if the whole thing were supervised by an invisible referee.

I will grant that the Germans invented quantum physics and psychology and moveable type and computers. Fair enough. I will grant that German is the language of science, of philosophy, of theology, of carefully crafted intellectual exchange. Like Latin, it is a language ideally suited to the university. But English—English!—is without rival as the language of magnanimous interruption. A Christian woman I met in Berlin told me she likes to read theology in German, but to worship in English.

English is the language of dialogue—that haphazard unpredictable grand good stuff of human speech. It is the language of Shakespeare and Dr. Johnson, of Hollywood and Huck Finn, of Jerry Seinfeld and Jane Austen, of Facebook and Faulkner and *Fawlty Towers* and the glorious tumultuous clamor of the local pub.

Grandfather

When I ask her what she remembers about her grandfather she describes the smell of pipe smoke, big spotty hands, a yellow-brown ashtray, striped curtains, a way he had of standing at the kitchen sink to make tea, the way he would speak, slow and precise, all the hard words brimming with mischief. She tells me about the day her mother promised her ice cream if she would stay home with her sisters, even though she had not wanted to stay home that day. When she thinks of him now, thirty years later, that is what she remembers most of all. How she had eaten the treacherous ice cream with her sisters, how she had betrayed him, how she was tricked into forgetting him, her grandfather, the day they buried him.

Horses

She complained that he is always distracted, off in his own world, emotionally distant, that he doesn't understand her anymore, doesn't really listen. It's as though you're not even here, she said. When she told him one night that she wanted a divorce, he worried for weeks afterwards, wondering why she wanted the horse, wondering how they could afford it, how they would feed and groom it, whether it would need to be vaccinated, where it would sleep on cold nights, where they would ride it and how often, and whether she really wanted the horse—or if the horse signified something deeper, some repressed need, whether perhaps she was unhappy, whether she lacked companionship, whether he was no longer satisfying her, whether she had found someone else or was starting to dream of a new life without him, free and unbridled. They never spoke of the horse again, but from that day on he spent more time with her, went on long quiet walks with her, looked and listened attentively, ate ice cream with her in the park and, once, on her birthday, presented her with a lavish illustrated book on the history of artistic representations of the horse. She turned the book over in her hands, mystified, and asked him why horses, what did it signify, what did it all mean, but he only gave her a small knowing smile, and kissed her on the mouth, twice, and asked if she would like to take a walk, or to sit a while at their favorite spot eating ice cream in the park beside the lake where all the boats go by.

Ice Cream

One afternoon I was rambling around Melbourne's Italian precinct when I passed a gelato bar. Tubs of gelato glistened invitingly behind the glass, bright and varied like flowers in a brilliant bouquet. It was the wrong time of day for ice cream. A gloomy Melbourne chill had started to gather, and I was already pulling my coat tight against the cold, but I found myself drawn irresistibly inside, towards the bright display.

Pistachio, lemon, chocolate orange, caramelized fig, rum raisin, green apple, blood orange, bacio.... I made a provisional review of the colors and flavors. Then, determined not to waste another moment, I resolved to begin the solemn business of flavor sampling. "I'd like to try the melon and the dark chocolate," I said to the girl behind the counter, who had been waiting with benign attentiveness.

"I'm sorry," she said. "One sample per customer." She pointed with tight-lipped authority to a sign on the counter that confirmed this ominous stipulation. The sign was laminated on a white card. The capital letters glowered at me in a stark juridical font.

"One sample?" I said, a little unsettled. "But how can I tell which flavor I want, if I only get one sample?"

"I'm sorry, one sample per customer."

"But don't you see?" I said, smiling gregariously. "Unless I try *two* flavors—at least two—how can I choose the one I prefer?"

She shrugged, peering down at me like a judge from the bench, all kindliness and good intentions, but ultimately powerless before her own ineluctable proceedings. "I'm really sorry, but nobody's allowed more than one sample. It's the rule."

Now, as everyone knows, tasting different flavors is one of the principal joys of visiting a gelateria. The samples not only serve an aesthetic purpose, they also have important psychological benefits: the comparison of flavors allows you to make a final decision free of the burden of Menu Anxiety (and its grim corollary, Menu Regret). On this occasion, however, things were getting difficult. Under these circumstances, the choice of a sample was itself rapidly descending into all the consternation of an actual Decision.

Mustering my inner resources, I told her I would try the melon. She handed me the tiny plastic spoon with its reluctant globule of pale green ice cream. Nervously but hopefully, I tasted it.

I didn't like it.

Trying hard to conceal my growing alarm, I said to the girl, "I'm afraid I don't like the melon. What do I do now?"

She smiled sympathetically, all innocence, and raised her eyebrows, waiting for me to place my order. "Could I perhaps try just *one* more?" I said. "Don't you see that I can't choose *any* flavor if all I've tasted is something I don't like?"

"One sample per customer."

Stirred by her apparent misunderstanding, I looked at her passionately, full in the face, appealing to her not as a gelato girl but as a fellow human being. "But don't you see," I said warmly, "it makes no sense to provide one sample! It's just the same as providing no samples at all! I'm sure I would love many of these flavors—oh so many—but at the moment, all I know is that I *don't* like the melon. Really, if you could let me try just one more, just the caramelized fig . . ."

Half smiling, she said, "Honestly, I'd love to let you try another flavor"—but then furrowed her brow—"but if I let *you* have another sample, I'd have to let *everyone* do it." Her voice rose triumphantly as she tightened the knot of that invincible Kantian logic, that gelatogorical imperative.

Believe me, I know better than to argue with a Kantian. I thanked her and ordered two scoops of strawberry. I have no complaint at all about the strawberry. (Admittedly it was not altogether what I had in mind, but that is beside the point—yes, I admit it, the cream was a little too heavy, the flavor a little too sweet; to be perfectly honest there was even a hint of coarseness, which I deplore in gelato.) But as I made my way down the darkening street, more or less happy with plastic spoon in hand, I imagined my gelato girl returning dutifully to her work, quietly satisfied that once again the law had been upheld—not merely the law of ice cream, but that eternal law by which all things in heaven and on earth are held in balance and by which the threatening tides of chaos are kept at bay.

"Enjoy your strawberry ice cream," I imagined her telling me. "It is for your own good. It is for the good of the world."

❧

So I'm just getting to the end of my shift—I don't mean the bookstore, that's weekends; on Thursdays I help out at dad's shop. I'm nearly finished for the night, and this guy walks in, all loud and scruffy, waving his arms and talking about how much he loves ice cream, on and on and on, while I'm standing there smiling like a dumbass waiting for him to order.

Twenty minutes till I'm out of here. I hope dad arrives early, I'm dying for a smoke. Typical Thursday—splitting headache, feet are killing me, fingers are puffy from six hours scooping gelato. I'm meeting my supervisor in the morning. Starting to panic. She thinks I'm losing my grip on the thesis, she doesn't say it, but I can tell she thinks it.

This guy's still mumbling about the gelato. He could really use a haircut, reminds me of one of my weedy tomato plants at home. I ask if he'd like to try a sample. Oh yes, he says. You should see him then: hands behind his back, leaning over, staring wide-eyed like he's never laid eyes on a tub of ice cream in his life.

My supervisor knows I've been stalling, finding ways to avoid her. I cancelled our appointment twice in a row, told her I'm writing—yes, it's really coming together—but I've got nothing, *niente*, not a single word. Dad would flip if he found out. He'd throw his arms out like Jesus Christ Almighty and bellow "The fees!" while mum would start crying before you can say P-h-D, moaning, "Every *cent* your father gave you—and *this* is how you repay us!" In dad's eyes, every bloody vat of gelato is a down payment on my glorious future. Putting me through uni, building my career one scoop at a time. Not that you can get a career out of a philosophy PhD. "The Ontology of Political Liberty in Isaiah Berlin." I'll probably still be working here. They can pin the degree up on the wall beside the coffee machine.

I can't believe this guy, he's still studying the flavors. If he had a magnifying glass he'd look like Sherlock Holmes at the scene of a crime. God I need a smoke. I tell him the melon is great, just to hurry him up. I offer him a sample and he says, "I'll try the melon and the bacio." So I tell him he's only allowed one sample—and now he goes all serious on me, starts explaining that he can never make up his mind about anything unless he has at least *two* options. Jeez, get a life. I give him a nice smile, try to calm him down. I tell him I'm sure he'll like the melon, made this morning, fresh local ingredients, whatever. He seems confused, mumbles something about choice, but I give him the taste.

After our last cancelled appointment, she went all cold and serious. She wants to see what I've written this year. "I want to *see* it, Julia," she said, stiff and Sydney-like, her lips as thin and pale as lemon sorbet. I promised I'd give her the whole chapter—you know, the one I've been talking about all year, on Berlin's *Two Concepts of Liberty*. So here I am, Thursday night, smiling and handing out gelato and hanging for a smoke and so sick with worry that I have to pray I won't throw up all over the rum and raisin.

Apparently Mr. Tomato Plant doesn't like the sample, now he's begging for another one. Honestly, some people have no self-respect. He tells me it's impossible to make a proper choice unless he has more options. I can't give out any more samples, but I tell him I think he'll like the chocolate. Everyone likes chocolate. But no, it's not good enough for *him*. I'm looking at the clock wondering when I can get the hell out of here, and he launches into a *lecture*, oh so patient and superior, explaining why there's some kind of logical inconsistency in giving out one sample blah blah blah. Who is this guy anyway? Probably a washed-out schoolteacher. Does he even have any money, I'm starting to doubt it, or does he just want to stand here all night tasting samples?

I think I'll need a strong coffee before I leave. If I start writing as soon as I get home, who knows, I might have something by morning. A whole chapter by tomorrow morning? Who am I kidding. What am I going to do. What am I going to *tell* her? I mean it's not as if I've been slack. All I ever do is read read read, tucked away in the library, burying my bedroom in index cards, articles, sticky notes. Every working hour is a merry-go-round of positive and negative liberty, individual and collective interests, value pluralism and conflicting values, self-determination and necessary conditions of non-interference. . . .

I can't believe this guy: he must have seen I wasn't paying attention to the lecture, so now he's switched tactics. Big puppy-dog eyes, wistful smile. Can you believe he's actually trying to *flirt* with me now? For a taste of gelato? *Dio caro*, I feel like giving it to him just to get rid of him. How can I type tonight with these swollen fingers? "I'm sorry, I really can't give you another sample—what if we did it for everyone?" They'll never pay off my fees if we start giving gelato away for free. I don't even know what the chapter's meant to be about anyway. I mean, I could start by saying that Isaiah Berlin's work is misunderstood whenever negative liberty is isolated from his analysis of values, especially situations of conflict between incommensurable values. That would be something—it would be a start. Finally! He's gone all sour and sulky, but he's finally chosen a flavor. Wasn't so hard now, was it? I scoop up the strawberry gelato. Maybe two strong coffees will get me started, after, oh God, a smoke. He gives me five dollars. I could start by saying that Berlin's analysis is pertinent today, when the idea of freedom is more and more viewed through the prism of private consumer choice. The strawberry flavor's no good today—dad spoiled the batch, but there was no time to start again—but I'm not breathing a word, gimme a break, it's only gelato. He takes the cup and spoon. I know, I'll start the chapter with Quentin Skinner's reading of the *Two Concepts*, that'll be a good opening. I hand him fifty cents change. Skinner, then Hayek, then right into Berlin. He turns to go, but then surprises me with a shy smile, almost as though—yes, as though he's *grateful* to have just one flavor instead of all the samples. He holds my eye a moment, then walks out in the night with his cup of bad gelato.

Finally dad arrives to close the shop. I stand out front and smoke a cigarette. Dad brings me coffee in a paper cup, black and strong the way I like it. There's a cold wind in the street. I button my coat. It won't be morning for twelve hours.

∽

Here is Angelo Papini, padding lightly across the room at dawn so as not to wake his sleeping wife. Here he is shaving over the chipped sink and bending to wash his face. His clothes are neatly pressed and hanging on the brass hook on the bathroom door. He dries his hands on the towel and walks down the hall to the kitchen and puts the coffee on the stove. Still in his slippers, he goes outside to get the paper from the porch. He stands a moment while the frosty Melbourne air stings his face and he breathes deep, looking at the sky. Clusters of damp pistachio-grey clouds crowd around the edges of the day. It will be damp again today, and sunless, Angelo Papini sees: not a good day for selling gelato.

In the life of Angelo Papini there have been three great loves: his daughter Julia, his gelato shop, and a red delta kite. Seven days he works the little shop, rising at dawn to make his gelato and closing the doors long after dark. Sometimes, after closing on Sunday afternoons, if the weather is right he drives two miles to Royal Park and stands on the grassy hill with the kite glancing from side to side in the sunlight and the long white tails fluttering in the wind.

Angelo Papini returns to the kitchen with the paper. He pours the coffee and makes a thick slice of toast. He spreads the toast with his wife's grapefruit jam and sits at the small round table with his breakfast and his paper. He notices the dirty plates and cups on the bench. Julia must have been up late last night. Sometimes she stays up writing. He wishes she would not work so late.

Julia is the cleverest person Angelo Papini has ever known. She is doing a PhD. She will be a doctor, a professor, she will give lectures and write books and have her own office in the university. Her name will be on the door, just think of it! Angelo Papini never finished high school, nor did any of his brothers. He never so much as dreamt that he would ever meet a person with a PhD. But Julia is startling, bright, inexplicable. She is writing a thesis, hundreds of pages, about a famous English philosopher named Isaiah Berlin.

After breakfast he reads the sports page a little longer and shines his shoes. You can tell a lot about a man by his shoes, Angelo Papini has always thought so, and in twenty-six years he has never worked a day at the gelateria with dirty shoes. When they came here in 1966 his father did not have two pennies to rub together. He went out every day to look for work and came back every night looking broken and sad. But he was never seen on the streets of Melbourne with scuffed shoes; he shined them every morning after breakfast. Young Angelo Papini, the oldest son, saw all this.

Julia is finding it hard to write her thesis. At first when she talked about Isaiah Berlin her eyes would shine, big and bright like the high white windows in St. Francis' Church during a summer morning Mass. The talking made her light and beautiful, a kite in sunlight. This is why Angelo Papini loves his daughter's studies. Lately though she has stopped talking about Isaiah Berlin. She broods. She locks herself away in her room. She has taken up smoking, though it made her mother cry. Angelo Papini used to ask about the writing—*how is the writing?*—and she always said it is good, really good. One day he saw that this was a lie, so now he never asks her, never says a word about Isaiah Berlin. It must be very hard to write, he can see that.

Angelo Papini pads back to the bathroom in his slippers. He dresses in his pressed clothes and combs his hair. In the bedroom it is still dark. He takes the keys and wallet from the bedside drawer. At the back of the drawer, tucked down and safely hidden, is a grey library book. The book is

Four Essays on Liberty by Isaiah Berlin. Apart from the sports pages in the paper, Angelo Papini has never been much of a reader.

With his keys in hand he walks back to the kitchen and pours a glass of orange juice. When Julia was young, she would come with him on Sundays and they would eat gelato in the park and fly the kite together. He drinks the orange juice standing in the kitchen.

A year ago, one Thursday on his way back from the markets, he drove to the library and asked to borrow a book by Isaiah Berlin. Late at night when everyone was sleeping, he propped his pillow up and read *The Hedgehog and the Fox* by the secret glow of the bedside lamp. He read a page at a time, two pages at most. He had to borrow the book six times in a row before he finished it. He could not comprehend *The Hedgehog and the Fox*, and when he had finished it he borrowed *Four Essays on Liberty*. As long as he lives, Angelo Papini will never tell another person that he has read Isaiah Berlin.

Early yesterday morning, as he prepared the day's gelati, he found himself thinking about Isaiah Berlin. He added the sugar and thought: Does this mean we are free to make it alone, to make whatever we want of our lives? He mixed in the cream and thought: Does a person have such power over his life? He added the strawberries and thought: Can a kite be free if no one holds the line? With a groan of dismay, Angelo Papini saw that he had ruined the whole batch. He had not been concentrating. He chided himself, but it was too late to start again, and besides, there were no more strawberries.

He sits at the round table and pulls on his socks and shoes. He checks his watch. There are still ten minutes before he has to leave. He takes the dishes to the sink, rinses them. Glancing towards Julia's room, he is surprised to see the bedroom light on. She is not usually up so early. He puts the coffee on again and goes to her room.

When Julia graduated from her Honors year, Angelo Papini was the proudest of all the fathers at Melbourne University. He took the whole family to dinner—all Julia's uncles, aunts, cousins—and boasted loudly, bellowing the praises of his genius daughter. *And they have invited her to do a PhD! What a life she will have! She will be a professor one day! My daughter!* Silently, late that night, lying beside his sleeping wife, Angelo Papini wept— with pride, yes, but also something else, shapeless and big and desolate. He did not know how to name this feeling, not even to himself. He would think about it only one other time in his life, on that bright summer morning four years from now when, like a kite string in strong wind, the secret knot inside his chest pulled suddenly tight, and the steel gelato container clattered across the floor and he lay for several seconds staring at the ceiling in the stark unblinking light. During those last seconds, Angelo Papini would think about three things: the morning many years ago when his wife's neck smelled of fresh-baked bread as they made love in their kitchen; the day Julia had flown her first kite, ribbons of chestnut hair streaming behind her as she skipped and ran beneath the sun; and the way she had looked at him, seeing him stranded there amid so great a crowd, the night she graduated.

He knocks at Julia's door. She opens the door. She is still in her clothes from work last night. Her eyes are very tired, the color of blood orange. The knot of her hair has collapsed and straggles down around her face. The bedroom floor is strewn with the wreckage of her studies, books and notes and papers and unknown crumpled things. The air is stale with cigarette smoke. For a moment she is distant, distracted. Then she sees him.

He asks her would she like some coffee. She follows him out to the kitchen. Angelo Papini pours two cups of black coffee. They sit at the kitchen table. She tells him about Isaiah Berlin.

Joy

1

As icons are painted on gold, so the lives of saints are written on a background of light.

2

Evelyn Underhill knew a saintly man, Father Wainwright. "He was an indifferent—and in later years an inarticulate—preacher; people came to his sermons, not so much to listen as to look at his face."

3

Why are the faces of holy people so important, not only in iconography but also in Christian memory and experience? Joy is the physical surfacing of the light of God. As the moon is reflected on the water, so joy shines in the holy face.

4

Each thing shines with its own particularity, the irreducible strangeness of its difference. G. K. Chesterton speaks of "the startling wetness of water," "the fieriness of fire," "the unutterable muddiness of mud." Joy is the vision of each thing's shining, an awareness of the unbearably bright difference of every other thing.

5

A painting summons us to relish its lines and colors; a tree invites us to marvel at its roots and shadows; the body of a lover beckons us to draw delight from its hidden wells; young children demand that we face them as they play, so that the miracle of their difference will not be without witnesses. Left to ourselves we shrink inwards, anaesthetized by a drowsy solipsism. Joy is waking to reality; joy is salvation from the self. It is our startled response to the call of another.

6

Joy is itinerant and can be visited in many places, but its regular venue is friendship. Friendship is the love of difference. The face of the friend is the mirror in which the joy of one's own difference shines.

7

The subjective precondition for joy is not earnestness but attention. Attention is the discipline of active passivity, an intense concentration on what is there. It is what Simone Weil calls "waiting": "We do not obtain the most precious gifts by going in search of them but by waiting for them." This is why St. Paul speaks of joy not as aesthetics but as ethics. Writing to the Philippians in the chains of Christ, he gives them a moral imperative: "Rejoice!"

8

Joy is most intimately related not to happiness but to sorrow, not to fullness but to the void of non-being. Joy is ontological vulnerability, a leap across the abyss of difference. Sorrow is a small hole in the flute through which joy breathes its tune.

9

Happiness is analogous to joy as Facebook is analogous to friendship, or as a brothel is analogous to marriage. Happiness is the gratification of desire. Joy does not fulfill desire but exceeds it so majestically as to obliterate it. Joy is ascesis, the criticism of desire. The criticism of desire is also desire's purgation and renovation. Joy is the baptism of desire, its drowning and rising again. The fullness of joy is an ache of absence. "Our best havings are wantings" (C. S. Lewis).

10

As that which breaks desire and denies gratification, joy finds itself in a strange alliance with the tragic.

11

Joy resists articulation and control. It is always vanishing, always beckoning, inconsolable union of memory and hope. It cannot be grasped since its nature is to undo all grasping. What would it mean to possess joy fully, to hold it fast so that it did not vanish away? That would be resurrection: the shining of eternity in a body of death.

II. How the Light Gets In

Ladies

Anybody who was brought up, as I was, in the riotous joy and madness of Pentecostalism, will know something that ought to be obvious but is often overlooked: that what really sustains the Christian faith is not its ecclesiastical hierarchies, its scholars, or its salaried religionists, but its women.

One of the marks of Pentecostalism is the presence of strong women. You will find them in every Pentecostal church: praying in the spirit without ceasing; worshipping sadly or exuberantly, as though they alone must bear vicariously the whole burden of salvation history; consulting their thumb-worn leather Bibles, extensively underlined, annotated, committed to memory; issuing swift, infallible moral judgments; and all the time patiently inscribing their own faith on the souls and bodies of their children. (That, incidentally, explains the contrast in Pentecostal gatherings between the uninhibited expressiveness of the women and the absolute docility of their neatly dressed children.)

As a boy, I was told that the most important person in our church was not the preacher or the musicians or even the swaggering itinerant evangelists who so often darkened our doors, but Mrs. Loy, an 80-something (and later 90-something) Chinese woman who had devoted her life to prayer. In all the years I was there, I rarely heard Mrs. Loy utter a word, but every Sunday morning her tiny arthritic fists could be seen raised high in palsied worship, her balding head shining with spiritual goodness. Sometimes during worship she would deliver a message in tongues, and an awed silence would fall across the congregation like a blanket. To this day I don't know what those tremulous glossolalic homilies meant, but instinctively I knew—as everyone knew—that they were the most important things ever spoken in our midst. Not because we understood them, but because they came from the heart of Mrs. Loy. She was, I forgot to say, the pastor's mother.

Such women are the engine room of the church. To a great extent, even the formal power structures depend on their secret society, their prayers and prophecies and discerning of spirits. They exercise a tremendous social and theological power, even in churches where the official theology is repressive and the official power rests solely in the hands of men. All this is, as

I said, explicit and transparent in Pentecostalism—but isn't the same thing true in churches always and everywhere?

Here, perhaps, lies the explanation of a fact that is otherwise extremely puzzling. Why is it that churches always refer not to *women*, but to *ladies*—the "ladies' group," the "ladies' Bible study," the "ladies' morning tea," and so on? As far as I can tell, the church is one of the only remaining cultural institutions—another being the public restroom—that favors this quaint terminology.

But truths lie buried in language. The word *lady* comes from the Old English *hlæfdige* (literally "bread kneader"), a woman of high status to whom one owes obedience—the wife of a lord, for example, or the head of a household. In popular piety, the term was used to designate the Mother of God, "Our Lady," the one to whom our homage is due (in Old English, the Latin *domina* is translated *hlæfdige*). Looking down from the cross, Christ calls his mother "woman" (John 19:26); when we address her, she is always "Lady."

Is this, then, the reason for that curious ecclesiastical archaism, whereby women are addressed as "ladies"? Is this why an assembly of women is convoked under the fearful nomination of The Ladies' Group? Is this the church's subliminal recognition of where its own power secretly resides—not in the young men with their furious ambitions or the old men with their weary dignities, but in the calm eternal purposiveness of the *hlæfdige*?

For is this not the mark of the *hlæfdige*, the Lady, that she governs the whole household and makes every servant tremble, all the while indulgently allowing her husband the idle vanity of believing himself the sole lord and master of the manor? Are things any different in the church?

Libraries

1

The library is the most solid and enduring item in the whole apparatus of intellectual life. In time, our academic fads and fashions, schools of thought and indeed entire disciplines will pass soundlessly into the abyss of history. But the library endures. In fact it grows only stronger, driving its roots down ever deeper while the wreckage of history piles up around it. The library's sheer material presence testifies to its ontological priority in intellectual life. Ideas are fickle and intangible, they occupy no fixed location, but the library fills space and time with an imposing materiality. It is the mind's anchor holding fast beneath the storms of time.

2

When you think of librarians, you may imagine those bespectacled mild-mannered characters with their index cards and carbon paper and obsolete black-and-green computer screens. Librarians contrive for themselves this Luddite image. But they are in truth the most progressive and visionary figures in intellectual life. They are like bloodhounds, always hot on the trail of the future. Their demure appearance is a cunning disguise that allows them to perpetrate their radicalism all the more effectively. It is a camouflage net thrown over an armored vehicle.

3

Just look at the Google Books project, engineered by Google but executed by an army of visionary librarians. And now libraries in America, France, and several other countries are organizing themselves to out-Google Google by creating vast databases of their entire national libraries. These people could be running the world if they wanted to—and if they did not have to be home by seven to feed the cat.

4

At the same time, there is nobody more conservative than librarians. Their enthusiasm for constant change and reinvention springs from an even deeper commitment to what has been received from the hand of the past. The librarian is an angel whose wings are spread out in fierce and loving protection of the past, while her face stares into the eerie light of the future.

5

In all the world there is nothing more dangerous than a library. Within any library are the seeds for the overthrow of the world. What bloody revolution cannot be traced back finally to a library? Or to some book that lay waiting through silent centuries for the day when it would be unsheathed? The rule of silence—upheld in all libraries since time immemorial—is a ruse. It is the silence of a tiger crouching in the reeds.

6

More than any other institution—certainly more than the state or the judiciary—the library proves that meticulous structure and organization are not obstacles to social transformation but its embodiment, the muscles and sinews by which history stretches its limbs.

7

The library is also the safest and friendliest place on earth. More than that: the library is the institutionalization of intellectual friendship. Which of us, admiring a shelf laden with the thoughts of dead authors, has never felt that these books *love* one another, even as they love to dispute and declaim? When I was a boy I played hide-and-seek with my brothers among the stacks, while my mother slaved over her PhD. If history is a tangle of weeds and briers, the library is that commodious garden where children play and every flower blooms.

8

Library catalogues have their instrumental necessity, but they should be consulted only as rough signposts. Your real goal is to cultivate the art of getting lost in libraries, just as you might deliberately lose yourself in the backstreets of a foreign city. "Like a true maze, the library leads the reader to his goal by leading him astray" (Giorgio Agamben).

9

Nowhere is architecture more important than in libraries. Physical space is to books as oak is to wine: no mere storage facility, but a medium that interacts, by a powerful alchemy, with what it contains.

10

Every head librarian is (or ought to be) vested with virtually unlimited executive powers. The library is one of those institutions in which benevolent dictatorship is not only desirable but essential. The head librarian is the captain of a ship at sea: her word alone is law. The librarian is answerable only to the collection, just as the pope is answerable only to God and a ship's captain only to the devil.

11

Since librarians are responsible to the collection, rash culling should at any cost be avoided. There is a cathedral library in Hereford, England, where rare manuscripts remain chained to the shelves. This measure was introduced in the Middle Ages to prevent theft—and I suppose it had the added virtue of securing the collection against the rash temptation of culling. Some books may appear to languish neglected in the dust. But they are like the seeds of those palms that spring suddenly to life after lying dormant in the ground for millennia. Nevertheless, when it is absolutely necessary to cull the collection, the librarian should do it swiftly and with a good conscience. "Every branch that bears no fruit my Father prunes, that it may bear more fruit."

12

I know a woman who worked as a librarian back in the 1960s, when the novels of D. H. Lawrence were banned in Australia. The library's Lawrence holdings were kept in a locked filing cabinet, and my friend, a young woman then, was responsible for the key. One by one she secreted them away; during her lunch breaks you would find her stretched out on the grass smoking cigarettes and reading *Lady Chatterley's Lover* beneath the shade of wattles and the hum of bees. The moral of the story: librarians are sly animals. If you're nice to them, you might one day get a glimpse of one of those treasures that lie hid in every library, away from dust and prying eyes, secured by lock and key.

Love

1

I have observed in my own handwriting a peculiar involuntary tic. My capital E is normally executed with three strokes: a sharp L-shape, followed by two swift horizontal strokes. It is a crooked, abrupt, ungainly sort of letter. But whenever I write the word *Elise*—my wife's name—the E takes on a completely different form and style. It is executed with a single fluid cursive stroke; it is curved, almost elegant, like a back-to-front 3. It is the only time my handwriting produces such a shape. Under all normal circumstances, my E—like the rest of my handwriting—is a jagged, haphazard, Runic, pagan-looking thing. But just ask me to spell my wife's name, and that first grapheme is mysteriously transfigured into something smooth, Cyrillic, serenely clean and Christian. As though it were inadequate to assign to *her* name any regular letter of the Roman alphabet. As though she required her own distinct letter, without which her name cannot be spelled or uttered. As though my love for her were the sanctification of language.

2

Like the Name of God that rebounds silently away from human speech, so love transcends language and eludes the grasp of words. Love is like the trauma that imposes its own peculiar patterns on a person's speech. Love is the twenty-seventh letter of the alphabet.

3

Love escapes language, because love transcends the law. It is that towards which law is always reaching; it is that which law has never touched. "Love is the fulfillment of the law" (Romans 13:10).

4

Love is not desire, even though it appropriates desire the way a flame appropriates dry wood. To love is to desire the desire of another. Love is kenosis, love is loss, love is the purgation of desire.

5

The purification of love is the task of life and the purpose of religion. The Christian faith is an ascetic doctrine of life, because it is a doctrine of love and joy. "All true joy expresses itself in terms of asceticism, the repudiation of the great mass of human joys because of the supreme joyfulness of the one joy" (G. K. Chesterton). Love without asceticism is sentimentality.

6

The widespread sentimentalization of romantic love in our society is a casual defacement of the Holy. Our pop songs and romantic comedies and breezy one-night stands are the moral equivalent of scribbling your lover's name in a public restroom. Except that it is God's Name—for "God is love" (1 John 4:16).

7

The experience of falling in love is the emotional shock produced by a sudden reorientation of personal attention. But such an experience is not yet love. To sustain that attention over time, even at great cost, is what it means to love.

8

Love without time is an absurdity, like fire without burning. Love is a mode of attention stretched out across time. Love is the temporal direction of the self. Love is nothing else than a certain object plus devotion plus time. "Love is patient" (1 Corinthians 13:4). That is why "the choice between one potential love and another can feel, and be, like a choice of a way of life" (Martha Nussbaum).

9

Love is mostly failure. If we understood ourselves, we would repent of our loves as one repents of the most appalling crime. Love is so entangled with selfish desire that we cannot even clearly tell the difference; nothing but the day of judgment will distinguish wheat from chaff. God's judgment does for me what I cannot do for myself: it separates one thing, love, from everything else that I am and everything else that I have done. What I need, *all* I need, is judgment. I live in hope towards God's judgment, which is also God's mercy—the only kind of mercy worth the name.

10

The opposite of love is not hatred, but shame. "Love bade me welcome yet my soul drew back, / Guilty of dust and sin" (George Herbert). Divine love is the abolition of shame. It is hospitality, welcome, the healing of the wounded gaze. "Love took my hand and smiling did reply, / Who made the eyes but I?" Shame stoops down, looking inward on the self. Quick-eyed love stands up straight, face to face with the beloved.

11

God's Word is love. Simone Weil: "God created through love and for love. God did not create anything except love itself, and the means to love. He created love in all its forms. He created beings capable of love from all possible distances. Because no other could do it, he himself went to the greatest possible distance, the infinite distance. This infinite distance between God and God, this supreme tearing apart, this agony beyond all others, this marvel of love, is the crucifixion. . . . This tearing apart, over which supreme love places the bond of supreme union, echoes perpetually across the universe in the midst of the silence, like two notes, separate yet melting into one, like pure and heart-rending harmony. This is the Word of God. The whole creation is nothing but its vibration" (Weil, "The Love of God and Affliction").

Manager

At the blues bar on Wabash Avenue, the band has taken a break.

Out comes the manager, he greets us, a real Chicago greeting, he thanks us for coming, he apologizes about the drummer, he tells us the regular drummer was unable to make it tonight. Two nights ago the poor man's house burned down. It burned to the ground. He lost everything. He lost his drum kit, his family photographs, his record collection. He lost his two dogs. They died in the fire.

"And he loved them dogs, I know he did," the manager pleads, smiling. "So *now*," he says, "now we gonna pass round the Love Bucket." And they pass it round, a big old beat-up bucket.

The words LOVE BUCKET are taped around the sides.

I throw in a dollar. My donation for a bereaved musician, a man without a dog, a drummer without a drum, another lost soul in the city of soul.

The manager watches as the bucket goes around. Thirty years he has managed this fine establishment. Thirty years he has produced the Love Bucket (who knows where he keeps it?) and has made his sad appeals, night after mournful night. A thousand friends he has lost; a thousand houses burned; a thousand hapless musicians' stories told. He has widowed their wives, orphaned their children, incinerated their helpless pets. Tonight he smiles (don't blame him, he can't help it), but some nights, I am sure, he sheds real tears.

I love the manager and his Love Bucket. In the wake of his nightly charity, it is a wonder that a single musician is left, that a single building is left standing, that the city of Chicago is not all a smouldering ruin.

He gathers up the Love Bucket. It is (I can see from here) nearly empty. Only a few of us, the tourists, have thrown in dollar bills.

But the manager does not mind. The manager is good to us. He beams at us and gives us his blessing. The band comes back and plays the blues.

Mega

My curiosity got the better of me. I went along on Sunday to the big Sydney megachurch. They had it all: the uniformed man with a walkie-talkie who met us at the door and briskly ushered us to our seats, very CIA; the big arena with a black stage, colored lights; words like *vision, success, awesome, purpose*; pre-recorded advertising segments (last week's sermon was available on DVD for $14.95); slick businessmen with their glamorous wives and Rolexes; handsome musicians and voluptuous singers (I confessed to my wife that I was committing adultery in my heart all the way through "All I Need Is You"); the give-your-life-to-Jesus altar call; and, throughout all this, the disconcerting ubiquity of what Peter Berger has called "the Protestant smile."

As for the preaching, it was motivating, inspirational. The sermon's title (this is all true) was "Ten Kinds of People that God Can't Help." The idea was that you should "invest" your time in positive happy friends, instead of making bad investments in friendships with hopeless, unhappy people: "Why are you trying to help people like that when even *God* can't help them?" Best one-liner: "The Bible isn't a book about God's love for man, it's a book about man's love for God."

But for me, the most interesting thing about the service was the dominance of the screen. Every moment of the service, from start to finish, was broadcast onto huge screens around the auditorium. When the pastor spoke, he would address one of the many cameras. When the worship leader spoke worshipfully to the congregation, he would face the camera. Even the heartfelt altar call at the end of the service was issued imploringly to the camera. During the worship songs, the screens would be filled with the faces of all those gorgeously happy singers and musicians; then a camera would pan across the crowd of raised hands before cutting back to a shot of the worship leader's passionate sincerity.

What made this so interesting was that the lyrics were superimposed over these images. So if you want to join in singing, you have no choice but to turn your face away from the altar (if there had been an altar), away from the congregation, even away from the flesh-and-blood performers on stage. Participation in worship is possible only through the mediation of the screen. The entire worship service is orchestrated as a cinematic event. You take part by turning towards the screen and participating in its projected images of worship.

The Protestant reformers used to complain that the Catholic priest was "doing worship" for the whole congregation, standing in their place and performing everything on their behalf—and a similar complaint is often heard about today's megachurches. But the function of the screen raises a more interesting problem: not merely that the congregation is worshipping vicariously through the onstage performers, but that the entire worship event is actually taking place onscreen. Even the worship leader himself is not a direct participant in the worship event. The real worshipping subject is his onscreen image. The flesh-and-blood performer participates in this worship only indirectly, through a vicarious participation in his own projected image, a larger-than-life image that becomes the bearer of transcendence. Similarly, the congregation is involved in worship only through the mediation of the screen.

Visitors to Manhattan are often struck by the uncanny familiarity of their surroundings. The city has been so frequently depicted onscreen that the physical environment seems a remarkably faithful copy of this more-than-real world of the screen. "Look!" tourists exclaim. "It's just like *Ghostbusters!*"

In the same way, towards the end of the service I glanced down from the huge screen, and for a second I glimpsed the pastor speaking earnestly into one of the many cameras. It was strange to see the man standing there like that: a miniature version—touchingly flimsy and insubstantial—of the real preacher whom I'd been watching on the screen. I felt embarrassed to have seen him like that. I averted my eyes and returned my gaze to the big reassuring smile high above.

Mistake

Once I dreamed my whole life. I dreamed my childhood, the easy early years in the shade of frangipani trees, the joys of solitude and reading, the boring years of school in a boring town, the humiliations of puberty, the perplexing miseries of teen romance. I dreamed I loved a girl on my street, the girl with curly hair, but then I moved away, I met someone else and we were married, we made a home, we made children, we shared all the tenderness and drudgery of married life together. As the years passed we grew apart, our closeness became an intolerable burden, a slow suffocation, until one day I knew, with a breathless dreadful certainty, that I had married the wrong person. I saw that the only one in the world I needed was the girl on my street, the girl with the curly hair whom I had loved all those years ago. But she had long since gone away, she no longer knew me or remembered my name. When I woke from the dream, I lay in my bed beneath a blanket of despair. The truth of the dream was acute. It was unbearable. My whole life had been a mistake, one long sickening catastrophe, and nothing now could ever make it right. I heard the breathing of my wife next to me, and, choked by grief, I knew she was wrong, a mistake, the reef on which all my life was shipwrecked. Then she turned in her sleep, and I saw a single dark curl slide from her naked shoulder, and I saw that she was not the wife of my dream, but the other one, the girl from my street whom I had loved as a child, whom I had longed for, desolate and unrequited, in my dream.

Pan

One night when I was sixteen, our youth pastor preached a rousing sermon against the dangers of rock music. He informed us gravely that Led Zeppelin's "Stairway to Heaven" contained subliminal messages that can be identified only when the song is played backwards, or when a person hears it under the influence of marijuana.

Intrigued and hopeful, my Christian friends and I hurried off to put the theory to the test. And so we sat down with the album in one hand and a bag of weed in the other, eager to partake of those alluring occult messages.

It was in this way that the strange world of *Led Zeppelin IV* began to open itself to me. The album conjured up a world of forests and magic and spirits, of gods and fertility rites and the secret powers of the earth. There was, as Erik Davis puts it in his book on *Led Zeppelin IV*, a certain "wayward tantric magic" in the music. We were invited to enter the mysteries of primitive ritual, to "dance in the dark of night, sing to the morning light." The songs made us ache for a long-forgotten world, a world of sensual pagan magic that had been eclipsed by the cool rationality of Christianity: "Tired eyes in the sunrise, waiting for the eastern glow."

The songs promised a synthesis of the erotic and the religious, a convergence of drugs and mysticism, the awakening of a strange authentic "reason" that transcends the stifling limits of modernity. As "Stairway to Heaven" puts it:

> And it's whispered that soon
>
> If we all call the tune
>
> Then the piper will lead us to reason
>
> And a new day will dawn
>
> For those who stand long
>
> And the forests will echo with laughter.

It is the pagan god Pan, that horned and horny deity, who will lead us out from the darkness of the West into the soft eastern light of a new age. A return of pagan magic promises to restore the primal balance to our unhappy world: "the magic runes are writ in gold, to bring the balance back."

For Led Zeppelin, this call for a recovery of primal balance crystallizes around the image of the Goddess. "There walks a Lady we all know, who shines a light and wants to show." Or in the words of a later song, "Down by the Seaside": "show your love for Lady Nature, and she will come back again."

For those of us reared on the Bible and the imaginative resources of the Christian tradition, Led Zeppelin's pagan-sexual-telluric world was exciting and alluringly exotic. Our youth pastor was, I suppose, quite right to feel uneasy about a song like "Stairway to Heaven." After all, the song was a very beautiful challenge to the whole imaginative world of Christian faith. (I take it that this is the case in spite of the fact that one of the main sources of Led Zeppelin's lyrics was the Christian writer J. R. R. Tolkien: where Tolkien used mythology to reimagine the world Christianly, Led Zeppelin used Tolkien to reimagine the world paganly.)

If Led Zeppelin posed a challenge to Christian imagination, then I suppose the rock band won the contest. That sort of mythology has penetrated deeply into popular culture. Walk into any bookstore and you'll find entire shelves devoted to nostalgia for a state of primal innocence, the recovery of a primordial harmony between humans and the earth, reverence for the sacred feminine, romantic idealization of the country over the city, the quest to awaken a dormant inner self, and a relentless suspicion of those institutions in which Western Rationality is transmitted.

And you'll find those themes not only in *The Da Vinci Code* or New Age self-help manuals. Efforts in Christian theology, spirituality, and liturgical renewal are often guided by exactly the same commitments. Just think of those well-meaning liturgical experiments in which God is invoked as the Great Mother, or where the prayers and hymns celebrate (even while mourning the loss of) our primordial rootedness in the earth. Or just think of the way Christian teaching is calmly absorbed under the broader rubric of "spirituality"—as though doctrines of grace and Christ and salvation can be translated without remainder into the language of individual fulfillment and the inner life of the soul.

But where Led Zeppelin promised a renewed world and richer dimensions of human experience, the most striking thing about contemporary spirituality is its superficiality, its willingness to settle for banalities and prepackaged experiences in lieu of any deep reflection on the world or on the place of humans within it. Spirituality is a commodity: something to be selected and consumed by the privileged classes.

In hindsight, then, it seems that the most prescient lines in *Led Zeppelin IV* were not from "The Battle of Evermore" or "Stairway to Heaven," but from the autobiographical song "Going to California":

> Made up my mind to make a new start
>
> Going to California with an aching in my heart.

For all its sweeping grandeur and pagan vitality, the spiritual vision of Led Zeppelin leads finally here: not back to the forests, but to—California. The mysteries of earth, of magic, of sensual Lady Nature, of gods who play their music and frolic in the woods—all this finds its realization in the Hollywood spiritual therapist with her reassuring slogans, her smile on glitzy book covers, her wealthy and rapaciously unhappy clientele.

Led Zeppelin IV is good music, no doubt about it. I still enjoy as much as anyone its profoundly imagined world, its absorbing nostalgia, its alluring occult invitation: "the piper's calling you to join him." I understand this to be a serious invitation—but an invitation to be rejected.

Those churches that hope today to find sources of renewal in a quasi-pagan earth mysticism would do well to ponder the question whether Christianity can be so easily assimilated into the culture of therapeutic spirituality, and whether the promised "stairway to heaven" is finally anything other than a descent into the banality and boredom of the inner self.

Pocket

A dialogue

Wooden cross, how did you become so small, so comfortable to hold? How is it that you are just the right shape for my fingers, just the right size for my palm? How were your edges worn so smooth, wooden cross? Even my thumb and fingers feel better when they hold you. You are just right for my pocket, easy to cling to even when I am weak or very tired. You are so small that a sleeping child can hold you, little fingers folded around you underneath the pillow. Yet you are so strong that grown men, dying, have gripped you tight, white-knuckled, and never broken you. Were you really once a thing of death and horror, small wooden cross? Were you really ever something people dread? How could the terror of the earth be turned into such comfort, a thing so small and good, salvation in my pocket? What has happened to you, small wooden cross, to work this transformation?

Once, long ago, in the days of my heaviness, there came a man who saw me, picked me up, and carried me away. He whittled me down to size. He smoothed my edges. He held me on his back so that all may hold me in their hands, tuck me in their pockets, string me with beads around their necks and hide me close to their hearts.

Prayer

1

What is prayer? It is the eyes of the world looking back at God (Pavel Florensky).

2

Can theology penetrate into the mystery of prayer? Yes: theology burrows into prayer as the ant makes its tiny burrows in the earth's immense dark turning orb.

3

Once when I was sleeping, the sound of rain on the roof became, in my dream, the hammer of war drums beating in a jungle. A real sound, vibrating in my ears, echoed in the chamber of my dreams. In the same way, the vibrations of eternity echo in the chamber of our world when people pray.

4

Prayer is restlessness and silence and sadness. It is jubilation and a cup running over and the sound of all the gum trees clapping hands.

5

"We do not know how to pray" (Romans 8:26). The whole uniqueness of Jesus of Nazareth lies in this: that he knows how to pray, because he knows to whom he is speaking. His greatest miracle was not healing or walking on water or driving out devils, but teaching his followers to say *our Father*.

6

Why do we close our eyes to pray? Prayer is not a turning inwards, not a withdrawal into the silent recesses of the self. Prayer is open-eyed attention.

It is waiting all day on the shore for the glimpse of a rare bird. "You must wear your eyes out, as others their knees" (R. S. Thomas).

7

Nothing could be further from the truth than the notion of prayer as a spontaneous inner glow or an uncontrollable gush of sentiment. Prayer is discipline, order, hardship, habit, obedience. Whatever it is that makes up a life, that is what prayer requires.

8

Prayer and obedience are one. The monastery, that momentous institutionalization of prayer, is founded on this truth. In order to pray I bind myself to a rule, bend my will to another, submit to a grievous curtailment of the self and its demands. The vow of celibacy in many religious orders signifies this curtailment. There is some part of what it means to be human that is *crushed* in prayer. For the person bound to prayer, it would not be right to represent life as fruition, satisfaction, fulfillment.

9

At the same time, there is no greater freedom than the freedom to pray. Does God command us to pray? Yes—just as you might give water to a thirsty man and command him to drink. God gives us permission to speak to God: that is the liberty of the gospel.

10

A priest told St. Thérèse of Lisieux that she ought to feel distressed about falling asleep during her prayers. She said: "I am not distressed. I remember that little children are equally pleasing to their parents whether they are asleep or awake."

11

"There is a crack in everything; that's how the light gets in" (Leonard Cohen). The life that prays is an ontological fissure, a crack in being. In prayer, shards of light break through, and the creatures that dwell in darkness rub their dazzled eyes.

12

What is it that really sustains the church's life and witness? Our sacramental hierarchy? Our teachers and clerics? Our projects and resources? Our thick books of doctrine and law? Or is the whole church perhaps upheld by one old woman who shuts herself away all day to cry to God with sighs too deep for words?

13

God is color-blind. All that is wise and powerful and impressive blurs together; God can hardly make out the difference between them. Only the small, secret things are clear and distinct to God's poor eyes. The secrecy of prayer makes us visible to God. "Your Father sees what is done in secret" (Matthew 6:6).

14

We are always complaining about unanswered prayer. But if sometimes God doesn't listen, or doesn't hear, or doesn't answer, we ought to be relieved. The Lord answered Job out of the whirlwind—and Job was lucky to survive the ordeal. Nothing is more terrifying than the prospect of answered prayer. "For the sleeping god may wake some day and take offense, or the waking god may draw us out to where we can never return" (Annie Dillard).

15

Sometimes I think prayer is all that matters. Sometimes I hardly dare to pray.

Priest

Lord Christ, today I saw a priest of your church weeping, quiet and alone with a hand over his face. What was this strange, silent grief? Was it because of some failure in your people? Or some inadequacy in the priest himself? Is there something he needs, but still lacks, for his ministry? Was there something I could give him? A reading list, a bit of theology? Some encouragement and a friendly word? Or was it your own grief, the grief of your priesthood, that had entered his heart and broken it from the inside? When you wept over the lost sheep of Israel, was it because your priesthood was lacking, or because it was so full?

Christ our shepherd, Christ our pastor, Christ our priest, have mercy on all priests of your church. Have mercy on all who have responded to your call, even when their task is beyond all human ability. Have mercy on all who have to announce your forgiveness, even when sin's burden weighs heavy on their hearts. Have mercy on all who have to bring your healing, though they can command no miracles and work no wonders. Have mercy on all who have to speak in your name, though your Name is an unsearchable mystery. Have mercy on all who have to approach your table, taking your body in their hands, breaking it, giving it away to whoever wants it, a feast for the life of the world—even when they, your priests, are still so hungry and so poor.

Have mercy, Lord Christ, on all who feed others while they themselves go hungry; who pray for others when for themselves the heavens remain silent; who go on speaking your Word their whole lives long when they themselves have heard only the faintest whisper; who proclaim good news and pour out the oil of joy while their own hearts grieve—have mercy, and sustain them by the eternal Word of your joy and by the grace of your heavenly priesthood. Amen.

Psalms

Singing psalms. The problem, of course, is that we find ourselves singing about things that are quite remote from our own concerns. That's why we find some of the psalms so offensive: psalms of vengeance and rage and despair, for instance. We simply cannot conceive of such experiences, even though they are—manifestly—real human possibilities. When we come across those sorts of psalms, we tend to react with a bit of enlightened criticism, imagining ourselves to be morally superior because *we* have never felt that way. But we flatter ourselves. It is because we are so small, because we are diminished, that we have trouble with the psalms.

And the psalter is a cure for our smallness of spirit. Our own private griefs are, often enough, quite paltry: but we are invited to join in the gigantic earth-shaking laments of the psalms. Our own criteria for happiness are selfish and small: but we are allowed to share in the psalmist's magnificent heaven-rending joys. Our own love for God is so feeble that we might forget all about God for days at a time: but our hearts are torn wide open as we join our voices to the enormous lovesick longing of Israel's praise. We are safe, affluent, surrounded by comforts, untroubled by enemies: but we learn to join our voices to the psalmist's indignant cries for the catastrophic appearance of justice on the earth.

If a church sings only the latest feel-good choruses, its emotional repertoire will be limited to about two different feelings (God-you-make-me-happy, and God-I'm-infatuated-with-you). That is considerably less even than the emotional range of a normal adult person. It is why churches can, sometimes, seem strangely adolescent, even infantile: they lack a proper emotional range, as well as a suitable adult vocabulary. But in the psalter one finds the whole range of human emotion and experience—a range that is vastly wider than the emotional capacity of any single human life.

For a church to go from singing contemporary choruses to singing the psalter would be like seeing Shakespeare's plays after you had only ever watched sitcoms. It would be a shock to discover that human beings can be so *large*, and that they come in so many different varieties. Nobody has ever felt the way Hamlet feels, or felt so much: that is what makes Hamlet important.

We need the psalms the way we need Shakespeare. To make us bigger than we are.

To participate in the singing of the psalms is to enter into a pattern of worship that transcends private experience. When the church's singing is structured around Israel's psalms, there is a constant reminder that worship is not primarily a matter of personal choice; that religious experience is not primarily my own private experience; that the voice in worship is not even primarily my voice, but the voice of Israel, the voice of Christ, the voice of Christ's people gathered across time and space, collectively transmuting all the varied raw materials of human experience into the praise of God through the alchemy of Jesus Christ.

Revelation

The Revelation happened on a Sunday, on the evening of February 28, 1983. The sky was bright and clear that Sabbath night, almost supernaturally clear, as one TV weatherman remarked the following day. Scarcely a cloud in sight anywhere across the vast unbounded skies of the fifty states of America.

The conditions could hardly have been better for divine revelation. The Moral Majority was gaining momentum under the leadership of Jerry Falwell, a Republican was in the White House, the Southern Baptist Convention had passed a groundbreaking resolution on the vocation of women as homemakers, James Dobson had published *Dare to Discipline*, the godless philosopher Ayn Rand had died, the AIDS epidemic was judging the evil of homosexuals, and the Middle East was bracing itself to fulfill biblical prophecy on the plains of Armageddon. In spite of these obvious triumphs of righteousness, however, there were still some signs of wickedness in the earth. In fact, by February 1983 the stench of the ungodly had ascended up to heaven; the recent release of Michael Jackson's *Thriller* was, to those with ears to hear, proof that the end was at hand.

For many years now the evangelical lobby—galvanized by the alarming rise of secular humanism, evolutionism, atheism, and condom distribution, and by the decline of ladies' baking groups and prayer in schools—had carried out a tireless campaign for a public display of the power of the Almighty. At first the Lord of Hosts stood by his time-honored policy of mysterious concealment, encouraging the church to take responsibility for his existence by means of apologetic arguments and the publication of illustrated gospel tracts. But the Christian Right used its growing influence to continue the theological lobby until, wearied by their cries, their prophetic protests, their Saturday morning prayer breakfasts, the Rock of Ages resigned himself to the exhausting prospect of one last display of the glorious divine effulgence. This would be the Revelation to end all revelations, the full and final unveiling of the secret hidden since the foundation of the world, a Revelation to shut the mouths of the ungodly and silence the relentless clamor of evangelical prayer meetings. The church had demanded a sign: they would get more than they had bargained for. The eyes of all the nation would be dazzled. Once more the hearts of human beings would be lost in wonder, love, and praise.

And so it was that, at 10:32 P.M. Eastern time, the Ancient of Days rent the heavens, rolled up the sky like a scroll, pausing a moment for dramatic effect while the archangel sounded three pure notes on her heavenly trombone, and then bathed the entire American landscape in the pure unreflected light of eternal refulgence. It was a radiance to blacken the sun and blind the watching stars. It was, in a word, an irrefutable demonstration of the existence and power of Him Who Made Heaven and Earth.

There was only one problem. Nobody knows for certain whether it was due to an embarrassing oversight in heaven's event management, or to the cunning machinations of the Prince of Darkness, or to some deeper motive hidden within the divine counsel itself. Whatever the reason, it so happened that February 28, 1983, the Night of Nights and the turning point of the ages, was also the date of the long-anticipated finale of *M*A*S*H*. The epic three-hour episode was broadcast at 7:30 P.M. across the United States. It was the most watched broadcast in American television history. State and federal police statistics show that no crimes were committed on that night. Nor for that matter would any criminals have been apprehended, since the police, too, had taken up their positions around television sets at every law enforcement facility in the country. Nine months later, on November 28, maternity wards in the hospitals of America fell eerily silent. It is said that not a single child was born that day, since none had been conceived nine months before. As though no one had made love on the night of February 28; as though even the insistent drives of the body had been circumvented by the *M*A*S*H* finale.

On that divinely appointed night, the country's population had gathered one and all around their television sets, breathless with anticipation to see if Hawkeye would recover from his mental breakdown, to see if B.J. would get his longed-for discharge, to see if Colonel Potter would get the tank removed safely from the camp latrines, to see if Father Mulcahy would recover from his shocking accident, to see if Max Klinger would marry Soon-Lee and help her find her parents, to see if Charles Emerson Winchester III would get the job in Boston and if Margaret Houlihan would return to America or take up a position abroad; in short, to see the end of the Korean War—an event America had been dreading now for eleven consecutive television seasons.

So it was that, at the exact moment that the Glory of the Celestial Potentate filled the skies, viewers in California were tuning into the opening theme song, while in New York the credits had just begun to roll. Some later claimed to have seen a curious flash outside, though they thought nothing of it at the time. Others heard the sound of the archangel's trump, though it was assumed to be part of the show's dramatic background music. (In Colorado Springs, the trombone split the sky during the poignant and unforgettable scene where Major Winchester conducts the captured Chinese musicians in a performance of Mozart's Clarinet Quintet in A. The three heavenly notes neatly and harmonically punctuated the lyrical melody of the second movement, leaving all but the most diligent students of classical music unaware that this was an interpolation and not the work of Mozart.)

That is how it came about that the Revelation of the Most High and Holy One, which split the skies in a blinding flash from Long Beach to Long Island, remained unnoticed by all but a few astonished witnesses, small clusters of the homeless in San Diego, Boston, New York, Miami—persons who had, for whatever reason, been unable to find refuge near a television set that night and so found themselves wandering the streets alone, dolefully pondering the fate of Hawkeye and B.J., and gazing pensively at the sky at 10:32 P.M. Eastern time, the precise moment at which the Revelation of Divine Majesty pierced heaven and earth.

It was these dazzled vagabonds who, the next day and every day thereafter, roamed the condemned cities of America, spreading the news of what they had seen and heard. They were the sole witnesses of eternity, the ones who had seen the dawning of the new aeon, who understood that all the world's calendars had returned to zero on the night of February 28, that nothing would ever be the same from that time on. From stairwells and street corners and subway stations they proclaimed their solemn tidings and called for repentance and conversion to the One Whose Splendor Filled the Heavens.

But they were ignored or derided by the public, lampooned by scholars and church leaders, hounded and persecuted by the police.

They made few converts, except among the delinquent, the homeless, the displaced. They were lonely witnesses, though from time to time they would congregate under cover of darkness at bus shelters and soup kitchens to cultivate their prophetic gifts and orchestrate their strategies for the evangelization of planet earth. They grew their hair long and dressed in rags. They were rumored to feast on locusts and bourbon. They called themselves the Eyes of the World.

Before long certain false teachings sprang up from among their ranks. According to some, the Revelation had in fact been only the beginning, soon to be succeeded by an even more irresistible display of Heaven's Supreme Omnipotence. According to others, the universe had been obliterated on the Night of Nights, and the witnesses were now charged with preaching to the souls in prison, shadowy figures of the underworld who wandered the cities of the damned, eating and drinking and working and marrying, believing themselves to inhabit the land of the living though they dwelt among the dead, even their joys being, in reality, the torments of the grave. Others propounded the doctrine that the Revelation had not been a public display at all, but was instead a secret visible only to those few elect witnesses, guardians who must now protect the mysteries of their cult from all outsiders. Still others did not hesitate to conclude that Captain Hawkeye was the Antichrist; they declared that this satanic personality had been locked in mortal struggle against the Almighty since the dawn of time, in a colossal combat of darkness and light that would drag on, in bitter harmony, through all eternal ages.

Such theological aberrations were suppressed, and the witnesses continued to spread their teaching, preserving the sacred memory of the glorious Revelation. Even to this day they are troubled on every side, yet not distressed; they are perplexed, but not in despair; persecuted, but not forsaken; cast down, but not destroyed. They are condemned as mad, accused of disturbing the peace, charged with public drunkenness, loitering, harassment, urinating in bus stops.

But these charges against us are false, and our witness is faithful and true. We are the Eyes of the World. Among those who walk in darkness we have seen a great light.

Statement signed by: B. J. Miles
Address: c/o Harrison Avenue Homeless Shelter, Boston
Date of statement: December 21, 2016
Officer in charge: Daniel C. Stanton, Harrison Ave. Police Station

Sacrifice

My daughter handed me one of those big children's Bibles. You know the kind I mean. Set in a dour Protestant typeface and full of angry ink-drawn pictures of bearded Americans, stories punctuated by thunderous pronouncements from a Baptist-preacher God. The kind of children's Bible that has you scared to go to sleep, lest divine horrors swarm into your dreams or you are forced to wake, like Samuel, to the summons of that shrill and unfamiliar Voice.

She had opened it to the story of the binding of Isaac. She asked me to read. A horrible realistic picture showed Isaac bound to the altar, his father's knife raised above him, and in the foreground a white ram tangled in brambles. I had mixed feelings about how the story would be presented. Nervously I made the sign of the cross and went ahead and read it.

God's command to Abraham. Abraham's all-too-willing obedience. Isaac bound to the altar. The gleaming knife. The angel's last-minute intervention. The provision of the ram. The final triumphant act, knife dripping.

As I read all this, I wondered what my daughter, a sensitive girl, must be thinking. Was she appalled by the moral ambiguity of Abraham's act? Or did she see the story as Israel's critique of the cult of child sacrifice that had plagued the ancient world? Did she perhaps favor the Jewish view that it is not God who puts Abraham to the test, but Abraham who tests God? Or was she thinking of St. Paul's interpretation, according to which Abraham is willing to slay his son because he knows God can raise him back to life? Was she pondering Kierkegaard's searching analysis of Abraham's infinite resignation and of the teleological suspension of the ethical? Or Derrida's claim that the story reveals the limits of conceptual thinking as such, since duty and responsibility are inherently paradoxical?

There was a long silence. My daughter looked intently at the picture. The room grew strangely dark. Outside I could see storm clouds gathering. Then finally she shook her head and said: "Poor goat."

Saints

Karl Barth and Thomas Merton died on December 10, 1968. Barth died in his sleep at his home in Basel; Merton was accidentally electrocuted while attending an interfaith conference in Bangkok.

1

Brothers, you never met. But on Tuesday you stepped across the boundary and clasped hands, looking one another in the face and crying out in recognition. You lived by listening, that was your gift, that is why the world listened to you and loved you.

2

Brothers in solitude, yours was the hermitage of the writer's desk. You wrote your way into silence because there was so much to listen to. You kept your vigil, endured your life's long fast, because you were starved for words of truth (and in you the whole world hungered).

3

Brothers in the world, you heard Christ speaking in the silence and went out to greet him everywhere, even in unorthodox and unexpected places. You both admired Buddhism. Is it any more surprising to meet Christ in a Chinese monastery than in a cathedral?

4

Brothers in peace, you were afflicted by the violence of the world because you saw it rooted in your own hearts. When you raised your voices in protest against the world, you were always protesting first against yourselves.

5

Brothers in love, you didn't do too well with women, did you? You were perplexed by the way love can seize a life without asking permission or following the rules. But you never tried to justify it either. You knew that even our best gifts, even our loves, groan for redemption.

6

Brothers in death, one day the light that burned in both of you went out. In Basel, Mozart fell silent and there was no one left to turn the record over. In Bangkok, Buddhist monks sat with downcast eyes; all the stones were silent and there was no one left to listen to their silence. Outside, the sounds of children playing in the street. Bells ring. Two birds take flight.

7

Brothers in light, pray for us, for all our saints are gone. We made lamps but there is no one here to light them for us, and we have no oil. Was it our fault that we lost you? Was the world unworthy of what you heard and what you tried to tell us?

8

"But how do you tell people that they are all walking around shining like the sun?"

Showing

A homily

It has been said that one showing is worth a thousand tellings. Anyone who has been a teacher will know that this is true. Even the most careful explanation can fail to get an idea across: but one simple demonstration, and everyone understands.

This tends to be forgotten in the current debates surrounding atheism. When someone writes a book against the Christian faith—Richard Dawkins or whoever—right away Christians are tempted to start playing the same game, to fight fire with fire, to come up with even better arguments, theories, proofs. We have a peculiar innate fondness for winning. So we can easily forget that Christianity is, at heart, a religion of revelation, a religion of *showing*. At the core of our faith is no argument or explanation or convincing proof, but a simple act of manifestation—God showing us God.

That's why the saints have always been so important to the Christian imagination. We remember the saints, we celebrate them, we tell and retell their stories. The saints are important because they are human lives that have been transformed by their proximity to the divine life. They have become transparent, like windows, so that when we look at them we glimpse something of that other country, the strange new world of God. In a holy life, God's reality becomes visible. It's not easy to believe in God, not for any of us. But when we look at a sanctified life, it seems only natural to believe in divine grace, divine goodness, divine giving.

One such life is that of Henri Nouwen, a Catholic priest and scholar who left a brilliant career—he taught at Notre Dame, Yale, Harvard—to live in a L'Arche community among people with intellectual disabilities. L'Arche communities aren't merely care facilities. They are founded on the conviction that people with disabilities have gifts that the rest of us need, even though it takes a lot of patience to recognize those gifts and to receive them. In the 1980s, at the peak of his career, Henri Nouwen left behind his big book-lined office, his students, his fame, his prestige, and moved into that little community, where he would spend the rest of his life caring for the disabled and learning how to receive their gifts. Here was someone whose whole life had been defined by achievements in language—words, books, lectures—yet he turned away from those achievements and devoted his life to people who cannot speak, or whose capacity for language is painfully limited.

When we think of great lives, this is not the sort of thing we usually imagine. How can we account for a life like this? How can we explain it?

This is where the lives of the saints turn out to be so important. They are human stories that have no possible explanation—unless their explanation is God. They are lives that we can't make sense of—unless their secret is God. They are lives that we can't even begin to describe adequately—unless we invoke the name of Jesus.

I knew a person like this once, a man by the name of Mr. Goldsworthy. When I was young I used to visit him at a nursing home in Brisbane. He'd spent his life teaching the gospel, and in his old age he devoted himself to prayer and to caring for his elderly wife. Mr. Goldsworthy was a saintly man. He was the sort of person who could say one word to you, and you'd spend the next ten years thinking about it. I once went along to a church where he had been invited to speak. I knew he had been preparing his sermon for some time, and I was eager to hear what he would say. When it came time for him to speak, he stood up very slowly and faced the congregation. Then, with eyes full of tears, he spoke the words in a trembling voice: "Unto him that loved us, and washed us from our sins in his own blood." Then he sat down, and silence descended on the congregation. One verse from the book of Revelation. That was all he said that day, and it was the best sermon I ever heard in my life.

Long after his death, Mr. Goldsworthy is still part of my spiritual world. He remains present somewhere in the interior landscape of my heart. On one occasion, I remember telling him about some personal crisis I was experiencing—I don't remember what it was, but at the time it seemed important. I felt sure this saintly old man would understand, that he'd be able to answer my questions, that he would clear away my confusion, that he would know just what to say. After I had unburdened my heart to him, I waited for his reply. And then, instead of answering me, instead of saying anything at all, he just looked at me with those watery eyes and beamed a smile at me. I had taken my deepest concern to this holy man, and he gave me no solution, no explanation, no reply. Yet somehow that one smile told me everything I needed to know. It was a simple showing, and it was worth a thousand tellings.

Isn't that what we're called to do for one another? There are many among us—in our churches, our workplaces, our communities—who would like to believe in God, but somehow can't quite do it. There are many who would like to know God, but can't quite make the connection. Many people are acutely aware of the psychological and religious obstacles that make it so hard to believe (or to believe again). In a world like this, in a world where it's never easy to believe, God calls us to draw from the wells of God's own life and love, so that whoever thirsts can have something to drink. God calls us to show the love of Christ, to make Christ visible.

Jesus calls his followers not to be experts, but to be holy. He calls us not to argue, but to *show*. He doesn't say, "Let your arguments persuade others." He says, "Let your light shine before others, that they may *see* your good deeds and glorify your Father in heaven" (Matthew 5:16). The sanctified life, the life that has found its center in God, the life drawn from the wells of grace and joy: such a life is the only real apologetic, the only convincing argument for the existence of God.

What I'm talking about here is just the logic of revelation. Our contemporary atheists want nothing better than a good argument, a stirring debate about the existence of a hypothetical God. But as followers of Christ, when we talk about God we're not talking about a hypothesis that has certain arguments for and against it. We're not talking about a psychological technique for coping with life's difficulties. And we're not talking about a supreme being who is so infinitely remote that all we can do is peer through our theological telescopes, jotting down our lonely little observations and extrapolations. We're talking about a God who is already here, already among us, already revealed.

In Jesus, God shows us God. That is the whole secret of the Christian faith. Jesus is not God's explanation, not God's argument, not God's hypothesis. He is God's simple self-giving act. He is God's smile beaming at us from the depths of eternity. He is God telling us, "Here I am—for you." In Jesus, God shows us God. And that one showing is worth a thousand tellings.

Smile

1

The precursor of the human smile was the caveman's savage grimace (Angus Trumble, *A Brief History of the Smile*). The invention of dentistry is the only thing that stands between that threatening grimace and the polite social convention of the modern smile.

2

In the Protestant West today, smiling has become a moral imperative. The smile is regarded as the objective externalization of a well-ordered life. Sadness is moral failure.

3

Today the meaning of life is a stylization of happiness, the cultivation of lifestyles from which every trace of sadness has been expunged. Peter Berger identified "the Protestant smile" as part of Protestantism's cultural heritage in the West. In a Catholic country like France it is still considered crass to smile too often, or at strangers. Evangelical churchliness is the ritualization of bare-toothed crassness. Our cultural obsession with health, happiness, and positive thinking is a secularization of the evangelical smile.

4

The cultural triumph of the smile leaves behind a trail of casualties. Where Protestant churches theologize happiness and ritualize the smile, sad believers are spiritually ostracized. Sadness is the scarlet letter of the contemporary church, embroidered proof of spiritual failure.

5

When the church's theological rejection of sadness was secularized, sadness became a pathology requiring medical intervention. The medicalization of sadness is the final cultural triumph of the Protestant smile. If Luther or Kierkegaard or Dostoevsky had lived today, we would have given them Prozac and schooled them in positive thinking. They would have grinned abortively, writing nothing. The truth of sadness is the womb of thought.

6

Somehow the appellation Man of Sorrows attached itself to the church's memory of Jesus. The sinless humanity of the Son of God was manifest not in happiness or success but in a life of sadness and affliction. Erasing sadness from our culture, we also erase Christ.

7

"I was in Louisville at the Little Sisters of the Poor yesterday, and realized that it is in these beautiful, beat, wrecked, almost helpless old people that Christ lives and works most. And in the hurt people who are bitter and say they have lost their faith. We have lost our sense of values and our vision. We despise everything that Christ loves. . . . We love fatness health bursting smiles the radiance of satisfied bodies all properly fed and rested and sated and perfumed and sexually relieved. Anything else is a horror and a scandal to us" (Thomas Merton, in a letter to Dorothy Day, August 17, 1960).

8

I know a little boy whose mother had to go away for a few days. When she came home, he cried and told her he had missed her. Touched by his infant sadness, the mother said, "It's nice to be missed." He replied, "It's not nice to miss." It is nice to be missed because we learn what love means in the sadness of another. The face that always smiles is the face of a stranger. Love is written on the face of sadness.

9

I know a fellow who was interviewed for ordination in an American denomination. Asked to describe his hope for the church's future, his eyes filled with tears and he admitted, "I don't know if I have any hope for the church." Perplexed by his response, the ecclesiastical interviewers furrowed their brows, scribbled notes and question marks, conferred gravely about his fitness for ministry—though they ought to have asked for his prayers, poured oil on his head, sat at his feet and made him their bishop.

10

Where sadness is expunged from a society, the cry for justice falls silent. Johnny Cash carried darkness on his back, refusing to wear bright clothes as long as the world is unredeemed. Why do we dress our priests in black? Are they not in perpetual mourning for a world that is passing away? In a culture of happiness, it is all the more necessary that our priests continue to wear black, refusing the cheap comfort of bright vestments and the empty promise of the rainbow.

11

At the turn of the millennium, J. G. Ballard wondered how the next generation would perceive the twentieth century: "My grandchildren are all under the age of four, the first generation who will have no memories of the present century, and are likely to be appalled when they learn what was allowed to take place. For them, our debased entertainment culture and package-tour hedonism will be inextricably linked to Auschwitz and Hiroshima, though we would never make the connection." How do we explain the fact that Auschwitz and Hiroshima are immediately succeeded by the cult of happiness and the triumph of the smile? How can it be that the worst century was also the happiest? Our children will interpret our happiness as blindness and self-forgetfulness. We have drugged ourselves against history. Sadness is truthful memory.

12

Why are clowns so frightening? Their demonic aura comes from the fact that they never stop smiling. Hell is the country of clowns, where tormented strangers smile at one another compulsively and forever. The devil is the name we give to the Cheshire Cat that vanishes just beneath the surface of the world, leaving behind sinister traces of a cosmic grin. Human history is a record of that grin. Only the Man of Sorrows overcomes the world.

13

The Bible promises the end of history and the end of sadness: "And God shall wipe away all tears from their eyes; and there shall be no more death, neither sorrow, nor crying, neither shall there be any more pain: for the former things are passed away" (Revelation 21:4). This can be understood as an eschatological promise only on the presumption that history is catastrophe, a fall, a vale of tears. Sadness is overcome through cosmic redemption. A culture without sadness is a culture without hope. The cure for sadness is God.

Song

After dinner he felt so happy that he went into the other room and wrote a song, full of small words, monosyllabic gladness. When it was finished he brought it to her and said, Look, I wrote you a song.

She said, All this time you were so silent, I thought you must be angry with me, I thought you must be brooding, I thought you no longer loved me, I thought you were all alone, I thought you must be thinking of someone else.

He said, But I only think of you.

When she sat down to read the song, she was silent a long time while her heart within her grew glad and boundless as the heart of a child. Watching her carefully from the corner of his eye, he wondered if it was his fault that she had suddenly grown so quiet, so subdued, if he had done something to offend her, if she still loved him, if she had ever really loved him, if she was thinking of someone else, if she was all alone in her thoughts, alone beside him in the pale lamplight with the song of his heart in her hands.

Sydney

At five o'clock in Sydney the high-rises empty their contents on to the streets, people in suits blinking in surprise at the forgotten sunlight, everyone rushing to get someplace else or lingering to avoid it. On George Street I passed a woman with a spray can, doing portraits on big torn sheets of butcher paper. Someone handed me an ad for a Chinese restaurant or a topless bar, I couldn't tell which. I got coffee and stopped a while to watch a boy play a homemade guitar, his fingers conjuring aching Spanish music, as if by magic, from the ruined acoustic stump. I stayed for two songs, then someone in a suit called out a request for a pop song, and you could see the boy was humiliated but he played it anyway. I could hear the sad half-hearted improvisations as I walked away. At the corner a preacher thundered about Sodom and Gomorrah and the weight of sin that drags us down and drowns us one by one. A born-again biker, picture perfect with his beer gut and angry black goatee and leather Jesus jacket, he was hollering about judgment and repentance when his beady black eye fixed on me. He must have seen me there peering out from his beleaguered congregation. He saw me drowning in a sea of wickedness and threw me a lifeline, his gospel plea, *Have you sinned? Have you been born again, brother?* I looked away, pushed my hands into my pockets, hiding my sins from him there like stones, heavy and precious and inexplicable.

    Why do I shrink from the street preacher? Why do I hide from his piercing eyes and scuttle away and try to lose his voice in the consoling anonymous clamor of the street? As much as anyone else that day on George Street, I could only hope that he was wrong, that his implacable rage against the city is not the rage of God. But what if he's right? I was losing myself in the crowd, yet his words echoed behind me, something about *horror* and *wages* and *the pit*. What if he's right, and salvation means deliverance from divine hatred? Could I accept redemption on those terms—could anyone? Could I be born again? Or should I ask the preacher to lead me in a prayer of unredemption, ask him please don't save me, please let me stay in hell with all the rest? If Sydney is Sodom and Gomorrah, wouldn't it be better to stay and be swept away than to flee to the lonely mountains? Wouldn't it be better, for God's sake, to perish with all the rest? Could I explain all this to the preacher? Would God accept my testimony if I chose to bear witness in hell instead of heaven, if I loved the ones God hates more than I love God?

The preacher wants my sins. He is hungry for them, I can feel it at my back. Famished with righteousness. He would ask me to confess; he would suck the marrow from the bone. I caught his last words, *if you die tonight*, before his voice was swallowed up and lost in the noise of the city. I hurried down the steps to Town Hall station. Beside me on the platform two teenagers were making out. The girl's ear was studded with silver, her body pushed up against the handrail. A man with a briefcase was talking into his phone, sweaty and earnest, must have been a wife or mistress. I watched the bits of rubbish on the tracks and waited. I wondered if the preacher had been a prophet or messiah, if his words might be the last hard truth at the world's end. I hope I'll never see him again. Sometimes it's better to be damned than to be left naked without a name. Sometimes your whole life is just one dull tender sin after another, and you can't honestly repent of all that, not even if you wanted to. I buried my hands in my pockets, counting out my sins one by one like pathetic rosary beads as the man on the phone said *go to hell then* and the girl with the earrings moaned and the train rattled into the station, drowning everything in a monotonous grey thunder.

III. Younger Than That Now

II. Younger Than
    Then Now

Theft

When I was a boy I had an insatiable appetite for fantasy fiction. I read *The Lord of the Rings* when I was ten years old, and everything else I read was an attempt to recover the magic of that experience. I recall a few occasions when, as a teenager, I stole books. Walking calmly into the local bookstore, slipping a novel into my schoolbag, heart pounding in my ears as I strolled blithely out of the store, clutching my prize afterwards, giddy with anticipation and remorse.

There is a long history of book-stealing in the West. Alberto Manguel's delightful *History of Reading* (1996) includes a chapter titled "Stealing Books." He relates the argument of one seventeenth-century authority, that "stealing books is not a crime unless the books are sold"; and he recounts the tale of Europe's most notorious book thief, a nineteenth-century Tuscan aristocrat who had himself appointed overseer of all the public libraries in France. He went about his business with the greatest industry and enthusiasm, "dressed in a huge cloak under which he concealed his treasures."

Manguel observes that bibliokleptomania can be traced right back to the beginning of libraries in Western Europe, and indeed even further back, since the earliest Roman libraries consisted mainly of volumes that had been plundered from the Greeks. "Book thieves plagued the Middle Ages and the Renaissance; in 1752 Pope Benedict XIV proclaimed a bull in which book thieves were punished with excommunication." The pope's bull came too late for John Milton: his life had been devoted to books, but as an aging blind man he complained that his daughters were secretly selling off items from his library for their own profit. Then again, the pope's condemnation of book theft was strangely forgetful of one of the triumphs of Western Catholic tradition: I refer to St. Augustine's great work on the Trinity, which might never have been finished had not incomplete manuscripts been stolen and circulated in pirated copies among the unscrupulous monks of North Africa. Augustine was incensed; he had toiled over the work for many years and, horrified by the pirated copies, he promptly completed the work and had it respectably published. That is how the Catholic tradition got its most important theological treatise on the Trinity.

Admittedly, my own adolescent experiments in book theft were prompted not by a reverence for these noble traditions, much less by any poverty or need. There was something about fantasy novels (so it seemed) that demanded a more courageous means of acquisition than merely handing a few dollars over the counter. These were stories of knights, castles, magic, fabulous beasts: a routine commercial exchange seemed altogether too tame a transaction for such matters. The theft enabled me to participate more fully in the heroic world of those books: I didn't want to *read* the books, I wanted to *conquer* them. As someone has aptly said, "a book reads the better which is our own"—never mind the legality of the circumstances under which it was obtained.

Of course, the very mention of book theft strikes fear into the heart of librarians and all those whose lives are ordered around the collection of books. Who among us has not experienced the familiar scene: you loan someone a book; you ask them to return it in due course; it is (of course) never seen again. Your book is silently absorbed into the fabric of another person's world. If you were not a Christian you would hate them for it.

I once visited a medievalist friend who is a voracious book collector, and he offered to loan me a book. When he handed it to me, I noticed a faded note slipped inside the front cover, with the words: "I hope you enjoy. Please return when you're finished." My friend saw the note and remarked: "I'll leave that in the cover, since it was there when the book was loaned to *me*."

If you have been a victim of such permanent book-lending, you might want to adopt a more vigorous deterrent strategy in future. The library of the monastery of San Pedro in Barcelona was said to be inscribed with the following cautionary words: "For him that steals, or borrows and returns not, a book from its owner, let it change into a serpent in his hand and rend him. Let him be struck with palsy, and all his members blasted. Let him languish in pain crying aloud for mercy. . . . Let bookworms gnaw at his entrails in token of the Worm that dieth not. And when at last he goes to his final punishment, let the flames of Hell consume him forever."

Theologians

Thomas Mann said that a writer is someone for whom writing is more difficult than it is for other people.

I wonder if it's the same for theologians. Perhaps theologians are just people for whom the Christian faith is especially difficult, infuriating, and incomprehensible. Theologians are not, as a rule, especially talented or spiritually adept individuals. They are people whose minds have been hurt by God, and they are restlessly searching for—what? Healing perhaps, or catharsis? To expect so much from the study of theology would be futile. Yet there is no lack of opportunities for theological catharsis: often enough our worship services seem calculated to remove the difficulty of believing, to make God easy and accessible, more a cure than a wasting sickness.

Perhaps then we should define theologians like this: they are people for whom even the Christian liturgy does not provide adequate catharsis of the hurtfulness of God.

That is why you should try to show kindness to theologians. Not because they are exemplary personalities. Not because they are people of great faith. Not because they necessarily know what they're talking about. You should show them kindness because their faith is so weak and so vulnerable; because they are burdened by the difficulty of God; because they are driven to think about God the way some people are driven to drink. You should care for your theologians the way you would care for the widow and the orphan.

Jürgen Moltmann has said, "We are not theologians because we are particularly religious; we are theologians because in the face of this world we miss God." This does not mean theology takes place under conditions of God's absence. We "miss God" in the world only because God is revealed in the world, only because God is so devastatingly near. It is in the company of an intimate friend that one experiences the true depths of loneliness. Theology springs from the joy and the loneliness of God's nearness.

The proper goal of theology is not so much spiritual catharsis or intellectual mastery—clearing up every difficulty so that one can sleep at night—as it is the cultivation of theological friendship. Friendship sustains the difficulty of thinking about God. I warm myself by the fire of a friend's loneliness. God is near, and so we are lonely for God. Friendship is the small room in which we share together the loneliness and the joy of God's advent.

Theophany icon. Painted by Deacon Matthew D. Garrett; used by kind permission of the artist.

Theophany

On the icon of the baptism of Christ

Then, violent as an axe laid at the roots, a voice splits the silence of eternity and some holy thing plummets straight down toward the one who stands alone amid the flowing waters, whose life is purposive as running rivers, shunning the heights and seeking out the lowest place, rushing down so far and fast that our hands can hardly reach him, not without leaning dangerously near the edge, just as startled strangers once stooped to touch him in the manger and afterwards to feel his cold unyielding body in the ground, all his flesh exposed to the cleansing waters as he stands in silence, as low as any river's end, so that the baptist has to bend his starved body like a bow to discharge the quick sharp blessing, reaching down to touch the head of him whose sandals none is worthy to undo, as though he needed human blessing or approval, he, the benediction of all creatures, the still point around which all the worlds revolve, so that even the holy angels, bright in heaven's clothes and terrible beneath their wings of fire, lean hungrily toward his silence, poised beside him like runners before the race and clutching their robes as towels, having waited longingly through all ages for a chance to pay him menial honor (for eternity's immortal monsters covet meekness, lowliness, and anonymous service just as the children of Cain crave power, fame, and recognition), this mortal being who transcends them because he is beneath them, almost inaccessible in the extremity of his abnegation, and who might remain forever hidden from a world that worships power had not the voice like thunder announced his rank as firstborn of creation, and the birdlike lightning energies cascaded down upon him without measure, cleansing him whose touch makes all things clean, while the baptist's mad wild eye looks on in fright and all the angels turn their faces meekly down, folding their burning wings and bending with shimmering towels to dry his body in preparation for a second baptism, the funereal pyre in which the dove descends again as cataracts of flame, and what has fallen to earth leaps heavenward like tongues of fire.

Thirty-Three

There are some things I never really needed until I was in my thirties: Shakespeare, single malt scotch, the Daily Office, the *De Trinitate* of St. Augustine.

For example. The Shakespeare I was made to read as a boy—*Romeo and Juliet, The Merchant of Venice, The Taming of the Shrew*—was all spoiled for me. Even *Hamlet* is a play that I have never really learned to love, ever since I was forced to read it by an English teacher named Mrs. Morgan, who gave dreary afternoon orations about the archaic words and the imagery of rot and weeds and poison. Harold Bloom has said that Shakespeare will speak to as much of yourself as you are able to bring to him; and at sixteen years of age I was not able to bring very much, so *Hamlet* was wasted on me. Even when I read it today I am struck by nothing so much as a dull sense of familiarity, like meeting an old classmate you used to know but never really liked.

But then there are the plays I never read until my early thirties—*King Lear, Antony and Cleopatra, The Tempest*—and they are the great things, the plays that light up everything like stabs of lightning on the desolate landscapes of my heart. They speak to more of me, because I had more of myself to bring when I read them.

The other day I read *King Lear* again, a play whose every syllable seems charged with revelation, and I was glad I had never read a thing like that when I was a boy, back when I knew nothing of what a grand appalling thing it is to be alive, back when someone like Mrs. Morgan would have had to explain it to me.

We are always talking about the things we wished we knew when we were young. Important lessons are learned too late, and we feel that everything might have been different, everything better, if only we had learned those things twenty, thirty, forty years ago. But there are some things that it's good you never saw until you had a few lines around your eyes. There are lovely things that grow only in the desert, and there are truths that cannot take root in the fertile soil of youth but only in the harder, drier conditions of a life that has known disappointment and loss and the joys that come slowly.

This week I learned a truth like that, something I might have learned when I was younger, but am glad I never did.

I lay in the sun. I watched. I waited. I swung my arms. I looked back in fright. I felt the startling huge push. My head was filled with noise. I pushed myself up on my hands. I was very glad and very afraid. From beneath a great weight I dragged my legs up. I wobbled. I tottered. I—stood!

So it was that, at the age of thirty-three, at a place called Moffat Beach, I learned to ride a surfboard.

Thumbs

At Jackson he got on the train and sat across the aisle from me, and as the train started moving he leaned over and introduced himself. He was a seminarian who worked part time in web design. He worked in a church too. He said he reads my blog, that's how he recognized me. He asked how long I'd been in Chicago, and I told him just a few days, just for the weekend. I told him about the conference I was attending. I asked about his studies and he told me about his plans for ministry in the Episcopal Church. He was a gentle soul. I liked him. I told him about my family and our time in America. He told me about a paper he'd written on St. Augustine. I asked him to send a copy so I could read it when I got home.

We talked all the way from Jackson Station to Irving Park, never speaking, passing his phone back and forth across the aisle and typing with our thumbs, because of his deafness. Between us there was silence, even our tapping thumbs were silent, but our hearts were loud as bells.

Tigers

Two nights ago, my wife dreamt of tigers. In the morning she told me. A tiger bounding through the house, big and terrible yet innocent as a kitten, purring and growling with ferocious hunger.

I said, I suppose it is the dog.

She said, Yes, when he sleeps beside the bed I hear him stirring in his sleep.

I said, Like all dogs he dreams of hunting.

She said, The dreadful chase, the murderous lunge, the bloody feast and bones.

I said, He is never happier than in those dreams.

She said, And in my sleep I must have heard him dreaming, and so I dreamt of tigers.

The next night I went to sleep after a long sad day, and I dreamt I was standing outside on the grass as a tiger came towards me, his great paws pounding the earth like drums. I looked into the tiger's face and loved him, and I was seized by a sudden horror that I would be torn and eaten in one of his spasms of hungry unselfconscious joy.

When I woke I told my wife. Had I dreamt of tigers because of the dog beside the bed? Or was it my wife's slow breathing that I heard as she lay beside me, naked and dreaming of tigers, a dark tendril of her imagination creeping across the bed into my mind, her quickening heartbeat echoing like footfalls in my dream? Was it my own dreamtiger I saw, or hers?

Time

All my life I have loved libraries. When I was a boy, my mother did a PhD in English literature. In the afternoons she would take my brothers and me to the university library, and we would play hide-and-seek among the stacks while my mother leafed quietly through seventeenth-century folios, turning the pages with white gloves. I don't know what the librarians must have thought when they caught sight of three boys chasing each other up and down the aisles, hiding under desks, springing out from dark corners with whispered shouts. But I'm glad they never threw us out, because in those afternoons I learned to love the library, and to see those endless rows not as a gloomy graveyard of dead authors, but as a place of life and goodness and frivolity.

Sometimes when I found a really good hiding place I would pull down a volume from the shelf—one of those nice old cracked leather books, pages uncut, smelling of the eighteenth century—and I would turn the pages reverentially, scarcely daring to breathe in case the book crumbled to pieces from the disturbance in the air. I was ten years old, a boy. I was awed by old books. Awed by the realization that I would never have time in my life—that nobody would ever have time—to read all the books in the library.

That is how I came to see that there are things that transcend the limits of a lifetime, things rooted deep in time that will outlast me, that will go on standing at attention long after I am gone. It was a consoling thought. I have always been upset by the vulnerability of human life, and it felt safe and reassuring to be there amid those lovingly organized stacks, slipping the book carefully back into place, pages still uncut, and wondering how long it would be—twenty years? fifty?—before that book was ever touched again by human hands. And when someone finally cut the pages and read it, what mysteries might be waiting for them? What secrets might be revealed?

It was those afternoon hide-and-seek visits with my brothers that taught me that the library is a place of wonder, a place where I could snuggle in tight between the present, the past, and the future. The same book that I held had been handled hundreds of years before I was born, and would one day, after I was gone, be taken up again.

Here, in the library, time is so close that you can almost reach out and touch the past with one hand and the future with another.

Most of us experience time as a curse. In *Waiting for Godot*, Samuel Beckett said that we "give birth astride of a grave, the light gleams an instant, then it's night once more." Time is an intolerable burden, an insult against the human spirit, because it reaps us away too soon. But it was the library that taught me the true and Christian doctrine of time: that time is not a curse but a blessing. Hiding there among the rows of shelves, amid the benevolent smells of paper and old dust, I knew I was somewhere safe and good. Handling those old books, I loved time—or rather, I felt loved by time, as though those books had been waiting through silent centuries just for this moment, just for me.

I didn't know it at the time, but the peace of those afternoons in the library was a Christian peace. The happiness of my brothers and me as we scampered up and down the corridors was Christian happiness, Christian joy, the joy of time.

Together

Just before bed, I asked my oldest daughter what was the best thing that had happened to her all day. She thought for a long time and said, "When we read our books together." The best part of the day was the part we spent alone, together.

Violence

My children love adventure stories, and in their games together they recreate scenes from their favorite stories. In the comfort of the living room, in the darkness of the bedroom, in the eerie twilight of the backyard, they have been Peter Pan and a lawless ship of pirates, Bilbo Baggins and a terrible dragon, Aslan and the white witch, a scarecrow and a tin man and a cowardly lion; they have slain giants and battled dwarves and roamed beneath the earth and peered down on tiny cities from a soaring carpet.

There are people—mostly people with PhDs who have never met a real child—who think the old fairytales and adventures are too violent. Only an expert could think that what children really need is stories about tolerance, multiculturalism, sensitivity to difference, and all the abominable boredom of something called "life skills."

Anyone who has ever met a child will know that they inhabit a world of magic, monsters, and mayhem; that their freedoms and fantasies are loud, bright, and terrible as an army with banners; that what they really need are tales of giants and dragons, cruel strangers and enchantments, evil fairies and magnificent hordes of treasure, animals that talk and children that thwart their wicked stepmothers. They do not want to know how to be nice to a lonely old woman in the woods: they want to know how to trick her and shove her in the oven. Or if I may speak biblically, they don't want stories about obeying your parents and respecting your elders; they want a story about the youngest son who sneaks away from home and slays a giant with his trusty sling and five small stones. That is how children learn to navigate the dangerous rocks of the other country, that unimaginable foreign place where adults dwell; that is how they practice their moral agency, how they learn what it is to be free.

Our handwringing educational moralizers not only misunderstand childhood, they also misunderstand the relation between stories and morality. The teenager who brings a pistol to school one day and guns down all his classmates was not reared on the good honest violence of the old adventure tales, but on computer games where acts of violence occur devoid of any human context, any narrative of friendship, bravery, and noble deeds. He was also reared, let us not forget, on a steady diet of sententious animated films, with their paralyzing niceties of environmentalism, post-colonialism, tolerance, and Being True to Yourself. Our culture is blighted by the unprecedented mass production of such children's stories—not by people who know or admire children, but by film corporations with their focus groups, their market research, and their cynical cold statistics about what parents want and what they are willing to pay for.

Lately my children and I have been reading *The Silver Chair*, the sixth book in C. S. Lewis's Narnia series. It is a very good children's book, because it has all those things that children really love: talking animals, a strange unvisitable country, an evil witch, a hideous reptile, giants that cook and eat children, brave knights in glistening armor, enchantments of black magic, and, most important, the exhilarating absence of adult supervision, adult instruction, adult moralizing. It is a good children's story because it gives you not what children *ought* to like, but what they actually *do* like.

Today we read the chapter where the witch turns herself into a gigantic serpent, green as poison, with flaming eyes and a flickering forked tongue. The loathsome creature coils its body round the prince, "ready to crack his ribs like firewood when it drew tight." But our heroes rush at the snake with their swords. They strike its neck and with repeated blows hack off its head. "The horrible thing went on coiling and moving like a bit of wire long after it had died; and the floor, as you may imagine, was a nasty mess."

After we had read this edifying narrative, my little boy wandered off to talk to the dog, while my two daughters set about reenacting the scene in the living room. My older daughter dressed up like an evil serpent, while her sister and I took up our swords and pursued the vile creature across the room. The house was soon filled with all the blood and clamor of battle: the serpent's horrible hissing, the flashing of weapons, the bitter cries of triumph and defeat, the appalling sound of that evil neck being hacked in two.

That was when my little boy sauntered back into the room, carrying a handful of sticks and chewing on something he'd found on the ground outside. Amid all the brutality, the hissing and thrashing about, the blood-curdling shouts and warlike screams, he scratched his head and said idly, "Oh, are we playing Mums and Dads again?"

Virgin

Dear N,

Thank you for your letter and your questions about the virgin birth. I understand where you're coming from. Personally, I used to feel very proud of myself. I was up to date on all the latest historical arguments. I would smirk to myself when I heard someone refer to the virgin birth. I would make flippant remarks about Hellenistic mythology. Oh, I still said the creed and read the New Testament stories and everything—but I considered all this virgin birth business just a crude theological symbol, the primitive imagery of another time and place.

It is a very clever way of interpreting the Christian faith, to say that something can have theological meaning even though it never happened. As though the creed were a conjuring trick, a magical formula rather than a confession about reality, about how things really are in this world of ours. As though God might redeem the world through charming metaphors instead of through brute fact, the bloodiness of birth and death.

Who do I take myself for? Am I really so much smarter than St. Matthew and St. Luke? Am I qualified to correct the church's creed, the sum of the gospel, just because I've read a few books on the topic? Would my own personalized ready-made faith—in which everything is arranged just as I like it, and everything offensive is removed—really be an improvement on the faith of the church? Wouldn't I be like the proud young carpenter who, first day on the job, scorns the silly traditions of other carpenters and gets to work building his own two-legged table—only to discover that the rest of the world knew what they were doing when they made them with four legs?

I guess all I'm trying to say is that I used to be a lot more cynical and sophisticated than I am today. As one of our prophets has said, "I was so much older then, I'm younger than that now." Nowadays, to be honest, I'm just very grateful to be a Christian at all. Two-legged tables are fine, as far as they go. They can be very artistic in an urban, lopsided sort of way. But you can rely implicitly on the ones with four legs; that's the kind you want when you're sitting down in the comfort of your own home, day after day, a table just like the one your grandfather used, and just like the one your great-grandchildren will use too, long after you've left the world and gone to that big dinner table in the sky.

It's a good thing to be a Christian—I'm sorry to be so banal, but that's what really strikes me. It's a good thing to believe something you didn't invent for yourself. It's a good thing to have a certain framework, a story that tells you what kind of place the world really is, so that there are some questions that are already settled, that you don't have to go on wringing your hands and wondering about. It's a privilege, a real privilege, to be able to join your voice to the church's confession: ". . . and in Jesus Christ his only Son, our Lord, who was conceived by the Holy Ghost, born of the Virgin Mary, suffered under Pontius Pilate"—and all the rest.

If you ask me, a faith like that is as good as Christmas: as reliable as the calendar, but full of surprises too.

Yours sincerely, &c.

Water

I praise you, God of creation's joy, for this small town where we have stayed this week, for the beaches and the headlands and the sea and the house where we stayed together and were happy.

I praise you for sunrise at the beach (or just-after-sunrise: for we always slept, I praise you, longer than we'd planned). I praise you for the meal of fish and chips that we ate from paper trays as the sun was going down. I praise you for the seagulls that croak indignantly because we will not give them any chips, and I praise you for the pelican that drifts on the water like a fishing trawler and heaves itself into the air like a 747, fat and majestic, wonderful to see.

I praise you for the girls in summer dresses on the street, for the girls basking nearly naked on the sand, for the young men playing volleyball and running with their shirts off to show the world that they are young and strong, and I praise you for the old men in swimming caps who go down to the water even when it is very cold, and for the old women who walk their dogs and stop to greet one another beside the sea.

I praise you for the surfers and the kayakers and the stand-up paddlers, and I praise you for all boats and for all who love boats and who go out on the water. I praise you for the man who built his own houseboat and told me with a sun-soaked voice, "You have *time* for things on the water."

I praise you for the wide flat rocks where my children roamed at low tide. I praise you for my son who licked the glistening salt off the rock and said it tasted good. I praise you for my daughters' glee and horror when they found the crab in the little pool. I praise you for the terrible high rocks where we saw the teenagers playing, lying facedown while the waves swept over them (and I praise you that they were not swept away).

I praise you for the Aboriginal woman who calls the whales, and for all those hours I stared at the water hoping to see whales spouting, and I praise you for those two glad mornings when I woke from dreaming of whales, filled with gratitude that I had seen them even in my dreams.

I praise you for the lake where we paddled in the boat with my friend while the dog swam alongside, right round that little island. I praise you for the way the silver light shimmered on the branches that hung over the water, and for my friend who said it was his favorite thing to see. I praise you for the way the dog rested his face on the side when we brought him on board because of his exhaustion, because he had swum so far and so well. I praise you for the fish that I saw jumping near the boat. And I praise you for the fish my children saw when they had waited a long time for it, looking.

May your praise be always in my heart and on my lips. For life is not long enough to praise you; and were all the oceans ink and all the skies a scroll, it would not be enough to tell of all your goodness in a town like this, on a day like this, when the sun is in the sky and the water shines like glass, a mirror of your glory, God of creation's joy.

Words (I)

And there was one day beside the sea when I decided to say only what I really mean. For once I would not waste my words. For once I would not squander them on falsehood, argumentativeness, good manners. For once I would not rush to fill the void between myself and every other person with a flood of words. For once I would not use up my store of words on sentimental attachments to opinions and ideas. For once I would wait, I would listen. I would speak only the true words, only the words that need to be spoken.

And so I waited all day on the headland beside the little cemetery with its windswept sun-bleached stones tottering illegibly above the sea. I waited until the tide had come in and the hoop pines on the hill had turned black and all the fishermen and seagulls had gone away. And then as the gray sky deepened and the first stars were waking up and a black light rippled on the water, I opened my mouth and recited the fifty-first psalm into the darkness, and the headstones seemed to gather close to listen, and when the psalm was finished I waited in the deeper silence for the crosses to reply.

Words (II)

That is how it will be on the last day. A voice will be heard saying, *Lord, open my lips*. And all the dead will stand up in their graves to reply: *And my mouth will proclaim your praise.*

Writing

Writing and the fall

Angels have no need of writing—though Goethe's Mephistopheles is a writer. Jesus left behind no writings; nor did the Buddha. "It is not the healthy who need a doctor but the sick." Writing is for the fallen, for the soul cast out of paradise and lonely to return. When our first parents took the apple, God killed an animal and clothed them. Words are the bloody skins stitched together to cover our mysterious theological shame. In the shadows behind every book lie the skinned remains of some dead thing; its smell lingers in the library and in the writer's study.

Kinds of writing

There are four kinds of writing: bad, mediocre, good, and great. The difference between bad writing and mediocre writing is discipline. The difference between mediocre writing and good writing is editing. The difference between good writing and great writing is miracle.

Writing and editing

T. S. Eliot once observed that good writers do not necessarily write better than others, but are better critics and editors. Good writers cull the overpopulated paragraphs of their work. Like a farmer protecting the livestock, the writer lovingly separates whatever is sickly and infirm—then loads the gun.

Writing and discipline

The self has a tendency to leak. Left to itself, it loses all definition, becomes a shapeless puddle. Writing, like ritual, is a cast into which the self is poured. Writing is care of the self. "He who would not be frustrate of his hope to write well hereafter in laudable things, ought himself to be a true poem" (Milton). A book is a few seconds of inspiration plus a few years, or a lifetime, of discipline.

Writing and patience

Annie Dillard notes that some people can write quickly—just as some people lift cars, eat cats, or enter weeklong sled-dog races: "There is no call to take human extremes as norms." A person who could write a page every day would be one of the most prolific writers in the world, even if half those pages had to be thrown away. Writing is slow because truth is shy. You can't get close to truth all at once, but only by a protracted exchange of fumbling gestures, awkward silences, tentative questions and replies. The patience of the writer is the moral complement to the shyness of truth.

Writing and jealousy

Like cleaning your ears or singing along to Pavarotti records, writing is something best done in private. All writing is solitary. Even collaborative efforts are stitched together from smaller, lonelier units. All sorts of things—in fact, most of the things that really matter—have to be excluded in order to write. Like a drawn bowstring, the writer draws back from the world in order to pierce it more precisely. The selfishness of the writer is jealousy for truth.

Writing and kenosis

Writing is a craft of selflessness. The writer of fiction creates a character through generosity and kenosis: she withholds her own agenda, silencing her own voice to make room for the voice of the character. Writers suspend themselves to let something else be.

Writing and death

The biggest difference between today's writing and the writing of the past is that writers are no longer put to death. Even if authorial execution was not always common, the possibility of death was implicit in every act of writing. The zone within which writers worked was marked out by this juridical possibility. But in the West today there is no writing for which a person could conceivably be put to death. This alters the whole nature of scholarly inquiry. It is also partly responsible for the bloodless mediocrity of contemporary writing.

Writing and life

The widespread notion that life is more important than writing—as though writing were something I do when I'm not really living—owes much to this modern abrogation of the threat of death. To distinguish between writing and living betrays a deep misunderstanding not only of what it means to write but also of what it means to live. Some of my happiest childhood memories are of sitting alone writing stories. Was I writing, or living? The distinction is not only false but also heretical, since for Christians (as for others) the secret of life is disclosed in a canon of writings. Yet this heretical distinction is perpetrated whenever Christians expect their writers to leave aside their labor with words to attend to something more practical. St. Paul describes his letter to the Galatians not as a secondary description of the reality of the gospel, but as gospel itself, God's own personal speaking in the world. If there is any distinction between life and writing, it is only that writing is (or can be) a particularly intensified way of living. The same sunlight falls across the café window and the magnifying lens: the only difference is the smoke.

Writing and truth

The purpose of writing, says Wendell Berry, is "to keep our language capable of telling the truth." All the difficulties of writing—even the most pedantic labors over syntax and punctuation—are reducible to the problem of truth. All writing is lying, as Samuel Beckett observed. But writers want to lie their way into the truth, to vaccinate themselves against falsehood by injecting it right into the bloodstream.

Writing and thought

I write not because I know but because I want to know. Among scholars today, there is no error more pervasive than writerly Docetism. The Docetic heresy divides idea from style. It is the belief that one can have clear thoughts regardless of the clarity of their expression, or that one first has an idea which is subsequently communicated through the neutral medium of prose. But between form and content there is a mystical union of natures; to write well is to think well. Language is not the external adornment of thought. It is thought itself, the blood and tissue of the idea.

Writing and God

Did the Hebrew prophets write in order to record their experiences of God? Or might those experiences have occurred in the act of writing itself? Would it have made any sense for them to distinguish revelation from the language that preserved it? Did they not find the face of God touching their outstretched fingertips as they groped their way blindly through the doorway into the dark house of language? The tightly knotted bond between God and language is the secret truth of all writing. According to the Zohar, one binds oneself to God by learning to write God's Name, for the Name of God is the being of God. Writing and religion alike bubble up from this hidden primeval fountain of theological magic.

The end of writing

According to Gershom Scholem, some Jewish mystics taught that on the last day God will annul the Torah. All the letters will stay the same, but God will rearrange them into a completely different combination, a new-yet-identical script. This is the goal of all writing. It is the promise for which writing waits: to be simultaneously deciphered and erased, transposed from human words into tongues of angels, burned up but not consumed in the ecstatic conflagration of the Word.

Year

And then there was the year without prayer. Or was it two years? Three? Or five? I guess I lost count. Anyway, all that time I could not pray.

Don't ask me why, don't ask me to explain it. It's not that I stopped believing: not exactly. It's just that everything around me was a terrible silence, and any word, a shout or just a whisper, only made the silence echo louder. It's not that I had stopped loving: not completely. It's just that my heart was cracked inside me, and all the words seemed stillborn, choked by sadness before they ever could get out. It's not that I stopped trying: not quite. It's just that I *tried* to pray instead of praying. It is the difference between trying to swim and swimming, between trying to remember someone's name and saying it. You might come close, but in the end it makes no difference. In the end it is not a matter of degrees.

Sometimes my wanting to pray came so close to the actual thing that I could almost feel it. Sometimes I was thrilled by the feeling of almost praying, just as a child in water, limbs thrashing, thrills at the feeling that swimming is really possible after all, then sinks.

I said the words, of course—I don't mean that I never said the words. I prayed the Lord's Prayer, I prayed the Gloria, I prayed the Te Deum, I prayed the psalter, I prayed the Jesus Prayer and the Hail Mary and any other prayer that seemed serviceable enough, any prayer that seemed to work for other people. But it was like hearing a joke that you do not understand. Everyone else is laughing; you chuckle too, just to be sociable, but it sounds pretty hollow.

St. Augustine says that wanting to love God is already love for God. It is a beautiful thought, the thought of a saint filled with tenderness for the difficulties of ordinary believers. I have often clung to that thought and have hoped that it was true. In my year without prayer I wondered if the desire to pray might also be a prayer. I hoped so. But it didn't seem a very safe bet.

To pray—not just to want to pray but actually to speak a word, a single word of prayer—that's what I needed. But all the words were false, because my heart was false. The words I recited, good honest words, got twisted up somewhere inside my mouth. Like I was saying them only to avoid God. Like all my praying was really just another way of hiding.

And yet I wanted—I think I wanted—to be found. To be seen. To be known so well that all my words would be unlocked, with nothing left to hide or to protect, nothing secret, and then groping in the silence I would find that one true word, the good word I was always looking for, and would present it like an offering, a little thing, so small, almost insignificant: my prayer.

But I could not find, have never found, that word. Maybe this search, this groping about for words, this always-wanting, will be enough. Maybe the year without prayer will last until the end of my life, until the last sigh when all at once the true word is pronounced, a word that is something like acceptance, something like thanks, something like surprise, something like pure joy and pure sadness, total discovery and total loss. Maybe that last sigh will carry me safely over into eternity, into the bright abyss of the Word of God. Maybe that sigh will blend imperceptibly with the Word of God's eternity. Maybe both words will sound the same note after all. Maybe I will hear with new ears, and will find that all my life was just that note and nothing more, one sigh, one long unbroken word of prayer. Maybe the note will sound clearest of all in this year, my year without prayer.

Maybe that's when I will come to know that all along my life was hid with Christ in God. Christ who breathes God's Word out of eternity into time, and breathes one sigh, the truest prayer, back again into eternity. Christ who became as we are and groped about for just the right word to describe it all, and then, having found it, offered it up to God, a small thing, fragile, almost insignificant: his own life.

Epilogue

> Silence! the young girl said. Oh, why,
>   Why will you talk to weary me?
> Plague me no longer now, for I
>   Am listening like the Orange Tree.

—John Shaw Neilson, "The Orange Tree" (1919)

Index

angels, 100, 119, 135, 138
    their attempt to get your attention, 97–98
    their courtesy, 49–50
    their life in Chicago, 10
    their lovely wings, 49
    their wings again, viewed from behind, 76
    waking up beside one, 85
bicycles, ungodly vs. godly use of, 8–9
birds, 41, 91, 102
    how to draw them, 7
    their names, 18
    Pelecanus onocrotalus, 131
    watching them while driving, 22
books, 8, 10, 16, 33, 48, 52–53, 75, 76, 77, 104, 135
    chained ones, 77
    enjoying their bloodthirstiness, 127–28
    forgiven for writing them, 50
    killed for writing them, 137
    lovely old ones that smell so good, 124–25
    ones your school teacher ruined for you, 120
    showing them sympathy, 12
    sinister typefaces in, 123
    stealing them, 115–16
boredom, 127
    what to do with it, 13–14
    where to find it, 88

cats, 37, 108
    accidental death of, 51
    their role in preserving world order, 75
    what their eyes teach, 52–53
caveman, the reason he is smiling at you, 106
children 17, 25–27, 35, 51, 53, 67, 76, 91, 100, 108, 127–28, 131–32
    how to make them very scared and happy, 28
    poetical reference to, 102
    speaking harshly to them, 8, 40
    their judgment on the relative value of politicians, 25
    why they are dressed so neatly, 73
clowns, 38, 40
    spiritual interpretation of, 28–30
    warnings against, 108
crayons, their anatomical function, 7

dogs, 39, 40, 136
    amphibious, 131–32
    conversations with, 128
    death during house fire, 82; *see* fundraising ideas
    how they make life worthwhile, 52
    nocturnal life of, 123
    things I dislike about, 114
dreams, 29, 58
    disturbance of, 53
    in the car, 22

dreams (*continued*)
    of Christmas, 49
    of drums, 90
    of horrible things from the Bible, 100
    of hunting and chewing the bones, 123
    of librarianship, 39
    of life, 85
    of tigers, 123
    of whales, 131
    of witches, 42
drugs, 20, 52
    and other things I did at youth group, 86
    can make you happy, 106–8
    how vaccination can help, 137
    prescription for Kierkegaard, 107

erotic literature, its use by librarians, 78
evangelization, of planet earth, 98

faces, 15, 34, 45–47, 53, 67, 68, 81, 83, 119, 138
    compared to trousers, 26
    ones that appear in nightmares, 42
    ones that are stretched very wide, 7
    ones that won't stop smiling at you, 107–8
fundraising ideas, 82

goats, as substitutes for human sacrifice, 100

handwriting, how to improve your, 79
heaven, 3, 25, 34, 49, 112, 119
    how to get there during breakfast, 15
    stench ascending to, 96
    whether theologians ever go there, 49
hell, 34, 36
    and clowns, 108
    and library lending policies, 116
    morally preferable to heaven, 111–12
    where it is located, 3
    whom you'll meet there, 3
house fire. *See* fundraising ideas

ice cream, 28
    and philosophical debates concerning liberty, 59–66
    and rekindling romance, 58
    cruelty inflicted by, 57
    texture of, 60

libraries, 39, 62, 75–78, 115–16
    correct method of getting lost in, 77
    how they make you feel and why it's good for you, 124–25
    secretly borrowing from, 64–65
    why they smell funny, 135
love, 5, 11, 12, 26, 47, 52–53, 68, 79–81, 83, 85, 94, 102, 105, 110, 112, 125, 139
    falling in, 37
    falling out of, 38

margarine, not as good as butter, 52

preachers, 8, 48, 67, 73, 86, 99, 100
    on big screens, 84–84
    underage, 16
    what to do when frightened by, 111–12
puppets, neglect of, 40

quantum physics, not as impressive as pubs, 55

serpent, how to kill it, 128
spirituality, 86–88
    of bikinis, 131
    of freeways, 19
    of the English language, 55–56
    of hiding in libraries, 76, 124
    of maple syrup, 15
    of reading Shakespeare, 94–95
    of the trapeze, 29

theologians, why they need us more
        than we need them, 117
tiger, 76
    how to share him with your
        spouse, 123
transport
    by automobile, 22–24
    by bicycle, 8–9
    by boat, 13, 131–32
    by freeway, 119
    by perambulation, 19
    by train, 53, 112, 122

whales, the happiness they always
        bring, 18, 52, 131
whisky, scotch
    and Russian iconography, 47
    and Shakespeare, 120

www.ingramcontent.com/pod-product-compliance
Lightning Source LLC
Chambersburg PA
CBHW020853160426
43192CB00007B/908